A Practical Guide

Managing in a Downturn

Editor: Kate Sayer

Contributors: Margaret Bennett, Tony Elischer, Stephen Lloyd and Ian Oakley Smith

DIRECTORY OF SOCIAL CHANGE

Published by
Directory of Social Change
24 Stephenson Way
London NW1 2DP
Tel. 08450 77 77 07; Fax 020 7391 4804
email publications@dsc.org.uk
www.dsc.org.uk
from whom further copies and a full books catalogue are available.

Directory of Social Change Northern Office

Federation House, Hope Street, Liverpool L1 9BW
Policy & Research 0151 708 0136
Directory of Social Change is a Registered Charity no. 800517
First published 2009

Copyright © Directory of Social Change 2009

All rights reserved. **No part of this book may be stored in a retrieval system or reproduced in any form whatsoever without prior permission in writing from the publisher.** This book is sold subject to the condition that it shall not, by way of trade or otherwise, be lent, re-sold, hired out or otherwise circulated without the publisher's prior permission in any form of binding or cover other than that in which it is published, and without a similar condition including this condition being imposed on the subsequent purchaser.

ISBN 978 1 906294 35 9

British Library Cataloguing in Publication Data
A catalogue record for this book is available from the British Library

Cover design by Kate Bass
Text designed by Kate Bass
Typeset by Keystroke, Wolverhampton
Printed and bound by Page Bros, Norwich

The information and commentary in this publication covers the law up to 31 March 2009. It is intended as guidance only, and is not a full or definitive statement of the law. Reasonable efforts have been made to ensure that the information and commentary is accurate at the time of going to press, but no responsibility for its accuracy and correctness, or for any consequences of relying on it, is assumed by the Directory of Social Change or the authors. The information and commentary does not, and is not intended to, amount to legal advice to any person or organisation on a specific case or matter, and is not intended as a substitute for professional advice.

The law described in this book principally covers England and Wales, but insolvency law applies equally in Scotland. The law relating to insolvency is different in other parts of the British Isles and internationally. There are also small differences in charity law in other parts of the UK outside England and Wales.

Contents

Acknowledgements		iv
About the authors		v
Introduction		1
Kate Sayer and Ian Oakley Smith		
Chapter 1 Effective financial management		9
Kate Sayer		
Glossary		39
Chapter 2 Fundraising in an unpredictable market		42
Margaret Bennett and Tony Elischer		
Chapter 3 Legal aspects to managing in a downturn		60
Stephen Lloyd		
Chapter 4 Managing difficulties		81
Ian Oakley Smith		
Glossary		93
Index		98

Acknowledgements

We would like to thank the many people in our organisations and families who helped and supported us in writing this book.

Particular thanks go to Helen Elliott at Sayer Vincent, who once again helped Kate by reading and commenting on the draft text. We also would like to thank all the experienced fundraisers who generously shared their experience: Marion Allford, Anthony Clay, John Gray, Giles Pegram and Judith Rich.

About the authors

Kate Sayer is a partner with Sayer Vincent and has been working with charities for 25 years. She advises them on a range of finance, tax, governance and management issues, as well as auditing them. Her work involves consultancy and training in the largest charities as well as support for new and much smaller charities and social enterprises.

She is a member of the SORP (Statement of Recommended Practice) Committee, established by the Charity Commission to review the charity SORP. She regularly leads seminars and writes articles on accounting and VAT, as well as other topics. A new edition of *A Practical Guide to VAT for Charities* was published in 2008 and further revised editions of other titles in the series will be forthcoming.

She is a visiting lecturer at Cass Business School for the charity courses and frequently speaks on technical and management issues affecting charities.

Sayer Vincent is a specialist firm of consultants and auditors for the charity sector. Its work focuses on making charities more effective through improved infrastructure, reporting and governance. It helps charities with mergers, systems implementations and training. Charities appoint the firm as consultants, internal auditors or external auditors. Sayer Vincent also undertakes practical research to enhance the efficiency and effectiveness of not-for-profit organisations, for example through the Adaptive Performance Management Forum.

www.sayervincent.co.uk
svinfo@sayervincent.co.uk

Margaret Bennett is a director of THINK Consulting Solutions. She has 21 years' experience in the sector, gained as director of fundraising for WWF-UK and the British Red Cross and, since 1998, through providing strategic, fundraising, brand, management and organisational consulting to a wide range of charities and not-for-profit organisations. She has worked in the UK and in international markets, with INGOs (international non-governmental organisations) and local operations, and across a range of causes including poverty alleviation, conservation and health.

She has a very wide experience of all aspects of fundraising, and as director of fundraising she developed fully integrated income generation strategies and structures.

As a consultant she works extensively in the areas of fundraising strategy and leads THINK's international market studies. She is also a specialist in individual giving, with particular expertise in donor development, and the integration of low, middle and major donor programmes. She very much enjoys mentoring senior fundraising and communications practitioners.

She is recognised as a strategic marketer working in the voluntary sector, and is particularly committed to enabling charities to translate their mission and vision into a successful – and practical – marketing strategy, which supports and is supported by its operational programmes.

Tony Elischer is managing director of THINK Consulting Solutions. He has 22 years' hands-on experience in the sector, covering leading roles in national and international not-for-profit organisations and consultancies. He has been a consultant for the past nine years, working across a wide range of causes and organisations.

He is an internationally regarded expert on marketing, fundraising and creativity, having extensive experience of helping organisations worldwide with strategy, communications, fundraising, management and troubleshooting. He has worked on every continent, actively pioneering THINK's international insight and strategy work, engaging with not-for-profit organisations, funders, regulators and international umbrella organisations.

His consulting covers projects of a global nature, ranging from complete strategy development and individual fundraising technique introduction, to review and audits of market operations and new market entries. In the UK, he mentors several charity chief executives and directors and leads a wide variety of THINK's client assignments at a tactical and strategic level. He is particularly known for his creativity and originality in approaching fundraising opportunities and challenges. He is on the board of the journal *Non-profit and Voluntary Sector Marketing*, the Resource Alliance and is former chair of the International Fundraising Congress.

THINK Consulting Solutions is the leading international consultancy dedicated to not-for-profit sector marketing – strategy, management, fundraising, brand, communications and new media. As highly experienced senior practitioners with strong personal commitment to the sector, it offers a combination of intelligent thinking, creative problem-solving, and robust, workable advice and action plans. Its strategic and practical solutions are aimed at improving charities' efficiency, effectiveness and profitability. It works with major international charities, both at the centre and with national offices, and a wide range of large and small national organisations in the UK and Europe.

www.thinkcs.org
margaret@thinkcs.org
tony@thinkcs.org

ABOUT THE AUTHORS

Stephen Lloyd is senior partner with Bates Wells & Braithwaite London LLP. He has worked for charities and social enterprises for nearly 30 years, advising on a range of legal, governance and financial issues. He is chairman of CaSE – Charity and Social Enterprise Insurance Management LLP – a charity and private sector joint venture to deliver insurance solutions for charities. He is also chairman of the Centre for Innovation and Voluntary Action and a trustee of four other charities. Stephen was the co-originator of the idea that became the Community Interest Company. He has written or contributed to a number of books, including *Charities, The New Law 2006*, *Charities, Trading and the Law*, *The Fundraiser's Guide to the Law* and *Keeping It Legal*. He writes numerous articles and lectures regularly on a variety of topics.

Bates Wells & Braithwaite London LLP is recognised as one of the leading law firms in the charity and not-for-profit sector. It acts for more of the top 100 charities than any other firm and many more of the top 3,000 charities. It has developed this position by being involved not just as lawyers, but also on wider policy issues. It has contributed to the development of charity law in a number of ways, through pioneering cases such as the registration as charities of Charity Bank and the Fair Trade Foundation, the Environment Foundation and the Countryside Alliance Foundation, and also through its contributions to the Charity Commission's reform of CC9 (*Speaking Out – Guidance on Campaigning and Political Activity by Charities*) on campaigning and political activities and a variety of other topics.

www.bwbllp.com
s.lloyd@bwbllp.com

Ian Oakley Smith is a chartered accountant and licensed insolvency practitioner. He has some 12 years' experience in the not-for-profit sector, typically working with charities in financial difficulty, seeking recovery or restructuring solutions. He has worked for various funders to charities, for example banks and funding bodies such as Arts Council England.

He has experience in working with different legal structures (for example, industrial and provident societies, companies limited by guarantee and companies incorporated by Royal Charter) and has acted as administrator or liquidator for many registered charities, including solvent liquidations.

He is a 'Key Individual' on the Charity Commission's list of preferred interim managers and has acted in this capacity. He is a member of the Pricewaterhouse-Coopers' charities team and sits on the Committee of the Institute of Chartered Accountants in England and Wales Charity and Voluntary Sector Special Interest Group and the Charity Law Association Investigations Committee.

PricewaterhouseCoopers LLP has a long-term commitment to working with the not-for-profit sector. Its team of specialists provide assurance, tax and advisory services to more than 450 charity clients. It advises them on every stage of their life-cycle – from those starting up or reassessing their governance structure to more mature organisations perhaps expanding overseas. Whatever stage an organisation is at, whatever role it plays, the firm works with the team to find a working solution tailored to that organisation.

www.pwc.co.uk
ian.oakley-smith@uk.pwc.com

Introduction

The turbulent economic conditions since the autumn of 2008 undoubtedly will have raised concerns among boards of trustees up and down the country about the ongoing viability of their charity. Charity managers and trustees will be well aware that most charities are far from immune to the possible consequences of the so-called 'credit crunch' and the consequent effect on economic activity. While the consequences will, of course, vary widely depending on the circumstances of each individual charity, trustees should be prepared to address the likelihood of both increased costs and falling income in the current environment. For some, this will mean a tightened belt, while for others the consequences may be more severe.

A PricewaterhouseCoopers report published in December 2008 jointly with the Institute of Fundraising and the Charity Finance Directors' Group concluded that, in broad terms, a quarter of charities had already seen some negative impact on their income and expenditure, and some three-quarters expected to do so within the next 12 months. Furthermore, about three-quarters of all charities stated that they were taking action as a result. The Charity Commission survey published in March 2009 showed that '64% of charities with an annual income of over £1m are concerned that the downturn is going to affect future work'.

Charities run into financial difficulties for all sorts of reasons. This was the case even in the relatively benign environment in which charities have been operating for the past decade, and it is likely therefore that the number of charities facing financial problems will increase as the impact of the recession becomes felt more widely. Obviously, all charities will want to avoid the need to cease to operate, but sadly too many charities leave it too late and reach a crisis point such that the options for turnaround are limited. In some cases, a formal insolvency process is the only route available.

Why do charities fail?

The external environment has the potential to affect all charities, but some charities will survive where others will fail. A charity's operating model, coupled with its

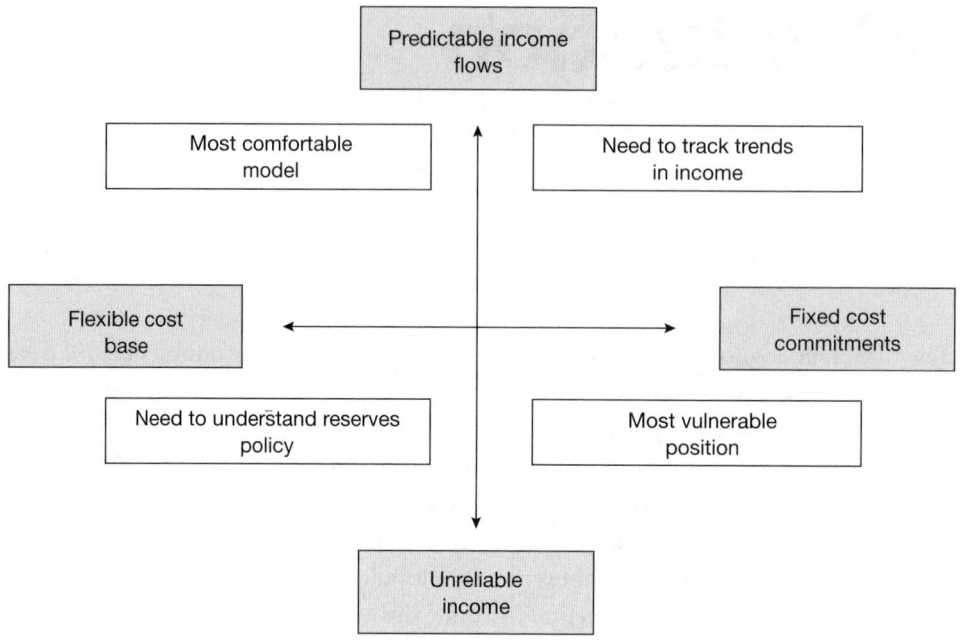

What makes charities vulnerable to failure?

attitude to risk and its reserves levels, will determine the extent to which it can absorb setbacks. The diagram above illustrates the balance between reliability of income and flexibility of cost base.

For example, a grant-making charity with limited overheads and controllable commitments is likely to find itself in the top left of the diagram. Such a charity will stand a good chance of remaining flexible in light of fluctuations in its income. On the other hand, a charity that is heavily reliant on restricted, project-based income, but has a significant fixed cost base (employees, premises, etc.) may well be in the bottom right-hand corner and may be less able to absorb setbacks.

However, while it remains true that a charity's operating model will render it more or less likely to fail, in practice, there is one common theme running through all failing charities – inadequate financial management. Put simply, poorly managed charities will be more vulnerable to failure.

Effective financial management

Effective financial management is important to minimise the chances of becoming insolvent in the first place, and should not be compromised. This is true at the best of times and vital in the current climate. When a charity operates in a benign environment when income and costs are easier to predict, it can often 'get away with' inadequate management, as funds are easier to come by. However, these inadequacies will be more exposed in a period when funds are limited and cost pressures significant.

The diagram below illustrates what we mean by effective financial management.

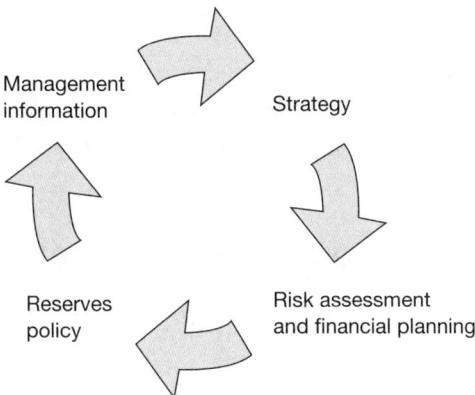

Strategy

Charities should have in place a long-term strategy to meet their charitable objects. This strategy should cover finance, operations and governance. During a downturn, it is imperative that the charity remains strategic in its focus. All options should be considered and trustees should not avoid difficult questions. Activities may need to be prioritised and even basic questions such as 'Can we survive as a stand-alone charity?' or 'Are we able to generate funds cost-effectively?' should be addressed.

Risk assessment and scenario planning

Once clear on the charity's basic strategy, budgets covering income and expenditure and cashflow, and balance sheet forecasts should be drawn up at a level of detail to allow trustees to understand the impact of the downturn and other risks on the strategy. Such detailed planning should take place for all realistic contingencies, for example 'What if our fundraised income declined by 20%?' This should enable the charity to understand – *really understand* – what it would do in the event of those contingencies materialising. This process of planning should not be underestimated: seeking agreement among the trustees on what may be very difficult decisions in the current climate will take time in itself, as not all trustees will necessarily have the same view.

Reserves policy

The charity's reserves policy will need to be reviewed in light of the scenario planning. If a charity has a risk-based policy already, then this should make life easier. If not, then now is the time to put one in place. The extent to which reserves are used to 'smooth' the effect of the downturn will be a key decision, as will the extent to which activities should be reduced further if reserves are insufficient to build up a reserve.

Management information

More than ever, detailed and appropriate management information will be vital to a charity's understanding of the extent to which the downturn is affecting its performance. The better the information, the earlier the charity will be aware of any issues and the longer it will have to implement a response. This is about optimising your charity's chances of surviving and prospering in this downturn.

Fundraising in an unpredictable market

During a recession the only certainty is that you will be fundraising in an unpredictable market. In such conditions, it is important to monitor the market, perhaps through the press, economists and emerging research, so that you understand what is happening. But don't forget that media hype is often not the reality of your donors' lives. After an initial period of concern, donors generally settle down until reality bites them directly, for example in the form of reduced income, employment uncertainty or rising household expenditure. And the point at which the media lose interest and move on to more interesting stories may be the precise point at which the recession is affecting your donors badly. Your priority is to see behind the media hype to understand the reality of what is happening in your supporters' lives.

Embrace change

At the start of a downturn, the focus is inevitably on worsening conditions, downward trends, and the need to protect the organisation from damage and loss. A defensive strategy may seem logical, and indeed by cutting back your investment you may avoid short-term losses and minimise your risks. However, if you maintain this defensive stance in the medium and longer term it will be counterproductive, leading you to miss opportunities and be poorly placed to take advantage of the market upswing when it eventually occurs.

The faster you accept that you are in an unpredictable market, the faster you can start driving towards it, as opposed to reversing away. Difficult times call for confident action. You will be able to assess and respond to the marketplace faster than the competition – competition that may be busy reversing.

Nurture your fundraising expertise

In a recession, you will need to call on your fundraising expertise as never before. Every day your 'rapid response' fundraising team will need to respond, decide and innovate. Every fundraising programme will need to be made to work harder. Every donor will need to be communicated with more intensely, more persuasively.

Your fundraising team is the driver of your fundraising, and if you reduce your investment in expertise you reduce your capacity to drive your fundraising forwards. In a recession, you need to drive as hard as you can just to stand still. To reduce your fundraising expertise in a recession is, therefore, a deliberate decision to reduce your income.

Focus on your core business

In an unpredictable market, the highest risks are related to areas of your business that are furthest away from your 'heartland'. For example, the donors for whom you are fifth choice, the donors who have been with you the shortest time, the fundraising techniques in which you have the least expertise. The last recession taught us that it is our 'core' business that is most likely to weather the recession, and that this is where we should be focusing our investment. Your portfolio should be diverse, but within the context of core business.

General fund

Make sure you understand your general fund needs. It is often the case that committed giving and general fund go hand in hand, but not always. General fund is crucial for the stability of the organisation, for paying your overheads and often for enabling you to accept major grants which do not cover their overheads. General fund gives you flexibility, fuels investment and enables you to be fleet of foot. Ultimately, general fund allows you to maintain your organisation even if you have to reduce your direct expenditure for a period of time.

Prioritise profit over growth

Big is not always beautiful. 'Doubling gross income in five years' is not the only fundraising strategy. Indeed, gross income should never be the focus of your fundraising strategy. The investment required to drive gross income growth – especially where recruitment is initially loss-making – will usually reduce your net income in the short to medium term.

Net income is the amount that is available to the rest of the organisation to spend on the mission and organisational overheads; maintaining net income should be the goal during a recession.

Put your greatest effort into keeping the supporters you already have. Develop the relationships you have with them, and aim to increase their giving. From the commercial world of marketing we know that it costs five times as much to recruit a new customer as it does to keep one you already have, and existing customers will spend up to ten times as much with you as new customers. This equally applies to donors.

Relationships with companies and trusts

Charities with a strong corporate portfolio or a track record need to hold firm and implement a new strategy to get through the next two years successfully. They need to prepare to emerge stronger and in a new shape for the future. Charities new to this area should look much harder at their cause and brand, and ask themselves whether they should revise expectations and scrutinise resource commitments in a very unpredictable market.

Increase the amount of communication you have with existing grant supporters; try to understand the challenges and circumstances they are facing; share with them how your charity is progressing. Strengthen your research to track and understand what is happening in the grant-giving market, as things will change quickly, with the potential for short-term opportunities to arise.

Legal aspects to managing in a downturn

The first thing to consider is the legal status of your charity, as the law relating to insolvency affects charities differently depending on how a charity is constituted. Charities operate under a great variety of constitutional forms, including companies limited by guarantee or by shares, societies incorporated by royal charter, industrial and provident societies, unincorporated associations or trusts, and soon the charitable incorporated organisation.

The tests for insolvency

There are two tests for insolvency under the Insolvency Act – the going concern test and the balance sheet test. The basis of the going concern test is whether the company can pay its debts as they fall due.

Under the balance sheet test, a company is technically insolvent if the value of the company's assets is less than the amount of its liabilities, including its contingent and prospective liabilities.

The effect of insolvency on different forms of charity

Charitable companies are normally limited by guarantee, which means the members will only be liable for the amount of their guarantee, usually a nominal sum of £1. The trustees do not have personal liability.

In contrast, the trustees of a charitable trust or the management committee of an unincorporated association are personally liable for the debts of the charity if it becomes insolvent. So if it has more liabilities than assets, the trustees (and possibly members) are liable to make up the shortfall.

Wrongful trading

Charitable companies still need to exercise care, however. Wrongful trading occurs when a company continues to trade even though the directors or trustees *knew or ought to have concluded* that there was no reasonable prospect that the company would avoid going into insolvent liquidation. Note that the fact that a company is trading while insolvent does not necessarily mean that the trading is wrongful, as long as there is a reasonable prospect of it not going into insolvent liquidation.

Practical implications of possible insolvency

The trustees must ensure that they have taken appropriate written legal and financial advice to show that they have acted responsibly. The trustees should hold prompt and regular meetings to show that they took matters seriously and acted with the interests of the creditors in mind. The trustees should also ensure that proper and detailed minutes are kept of all meetings so that there is an adequate paper trail to show how and why decisions were reached.

Treatment of restricted funds

How restricted funds held by a charity are treated in an insolvency is a difficult question. Charity trustees face the risk that they may be liable to make good restricted funds used for unrestricted purposes, as it could be a breach of trust. However, with little case law, it is not clear whether unused balances on restricted funds would be available to discharge the liabilities of the charity in an insolvency.

Managing difficulties

A charity may find itself unable to respond promptly to external factors, which could lead to insolvency. However, in the case of insolvency it may be possible to turn things round. First, the charity needs to know how severe the problem is. In particular, it needs to know how long it has before the charity runs out of money. The important issue here is remaining in control: if it runs out of money, then control may be taken from the charity by creditors or other stakeholders seeking to protect their position. This process may require a combination of deferring amounts due to creditors and obtaining short-term funding, either by selling assets or borrowing from stakeholders or funders. Cash is critical in this period, so every effort needs to be made to realise and conserve money.

A turnaround plan
Once the extent of the breathing space is known, trustees will need to agree a detailed turnaround plan. This will involve making an assessment of the various potential options and acting decisively to rule out those that cannot be funded and concentrate only on what is achievable. Time will be of the essence here. Almost by definition, a charity will have less time than is ideal to find a workable solution that is acceptable to all parties. Obtaining a consensus among the trustees may be a challenge, such that strong leadership will be required to ensure that inaction does not result.

Working closely with stakeholders and funders will be vital in this period. The charity will need to conduct its affairs with openness and transparency to ensure that stakeholders understand the full extent of the commitment they are likely to be asked to make and can contribute to what is possible.

In addition, keeping staff informed and motivated is very important. Ensuring key staff are retained in a period of uncertainty may be challenging.

Leadership and accountability are key
It is a fact that many successful turnarounds involve changes in management. There is a strong likelihood that the management team that allowed the problems to remain unaddressed for too long may not be the right one to achieve a successful turnaround, either in reality or at least in the perception of key funders and stakeholders. Most importantly, ownership of the turnaround plan often will itself be a full-time job. Consideration most certainly should be given to an additional, specialist interim resource, with the necessary experience and authority to lead the process

Trustees' responsibilities
Clearly, if a charity is seeking to turn itself around while it remains under threat of failure and insolvency, the trustees will need the comfort of knowing that they are not falling foul of their responsibilities and obligations. They may consider it wise to seek independent legal advice to confirm this.

Conclusion

There will be winners and losers during this downturn as with any other. Winners will have considered their environment, implemented good management, had strong cash resources and used reserves appropriately. It will be more difficult for charities to find solutions to problems in the current climate and the importance of avoiding problems in the first place therefore cannot be overestimated.

1 Effective financial management

Introduction

One of the characteristics of 'super-fit' companies is that they are able to take decisions relatively quickly and so respond effectively to external market conditions. Even if you do not aspire to being 'super-fit', you may find it helpful to consider ways in which you can improve your decision-making processes, as this will be a significant factor in your charity's survival.

Most decisions depend on the availability of information as a basis for the decision. The information needs to be appropriate – that is, relevant to the particular decision being made. It also needs to be recent information. Most decisions are looking forward and we are trying to use past information to help us make a decision for the future, so the more recent it is, the more likely it is that it will be helpful. We also need information of the right type, so for example, estimates about the future cash likely to come into the organisation may be more helpful than a schedule showing how much we have invested in the project in the past.

This chapter focuses on the financial management tools available to the charity trustees and the management team to help them have good-quality information readily available to support decision making.

Making sure your strategy is relevant

Many charities will develop their strategy for a medium-term period – say three or five years. As part of the process of developing the strategy, many charities will consult with their stakeholder groups, consider the external environment, and review their own strengths and weaknesses. The drawback to this process is that the review reflects the position only at the time that the review takes place. Many aspects of the external environment may have changed since the initial review to generate the strategy. Therefore, you need to have mechanisms to revisit the strategy in light of a changing external environment.

Scenario planning

Developing different possible scenarios will help the organisation to prepare for change in the external environment. Having talked about different possibilities, the trustees and managers will be more attuned to the early warning signs of change in the external environment, thus equipping them to respond more quickly.

Step 1

The first step in scenario planning is to consider whether your strategic plan relies on a certain view of the world.

> **Case study**
>
> Women's Health Centre (WHC) provides counselling and therapy for women. WHC has developed a strategy that assumes the following.
>
> - Society will continue to see some women's health issues as different from the general health requirements of the population as a whole.
>
> - Health issues specific to women will not be provided for adequately through the general health service.
>
> - Women will prefer to seek help in a specifically women-oriented environment.
>
> - Therapy is seen as an appropriate approach to deal with problems.
>
> From this we can extract two different world views that underpin the overall existence of WHC:
>
> - an approach that focuses on individuals as opposed to a view that it is the collective good that is paramount
>
> - an approach that values therapy rather than changing the basis on which society operates.

Step 2

Each of these approaches is an axis that we can use to build four different scenarios, allowing us to develop pictures of how things might look if we change the assumptions.

Case study – WHC

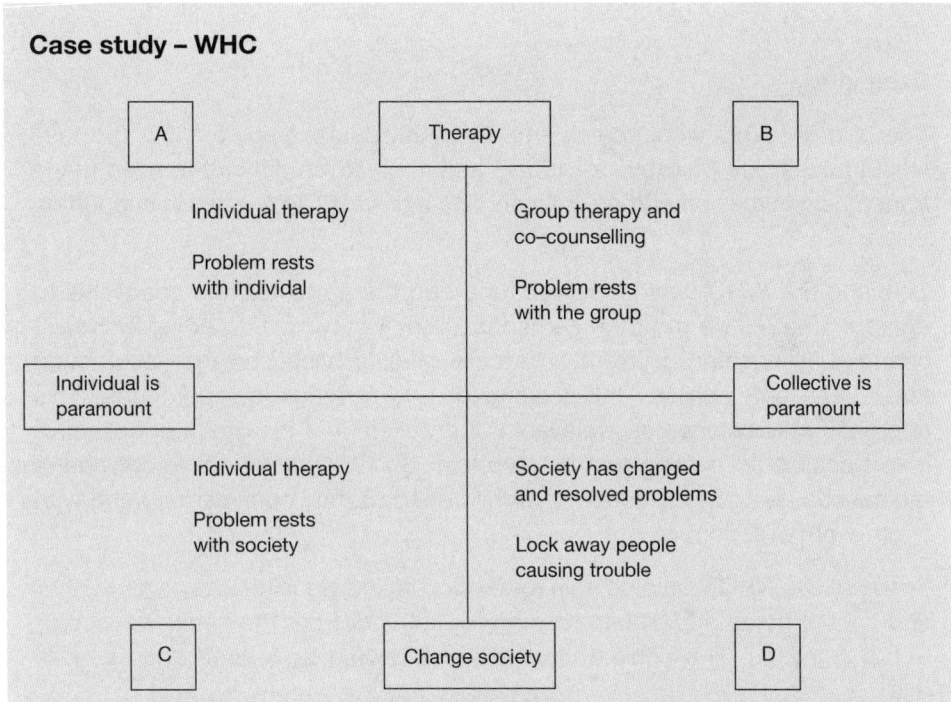

From this, WHC can see that it may have a role to play where the individual is seen as paramount (scenarios A and C), but that it may have no role where this approach is not valued. It may have some role in helping with group therapy (scenario B), but the collective view may also 'de-professionalise' therapy and see it more as a shared responsibility of the group. WHC would have no role in a society that does not recognise the value of therapy and treats anyone who cannot adapt to the new society as a troublemaker or even a criminal (scenario D).

Step three

Now overlay these different views with a changing economic environment and consider which approach is more likely. You can then start to develop responses to the changed environment and consider how your organisation will be perceived, how it would need to change its position and the services that it offers.

> **Case study**
>
> Scenario A – WHC would be able to offer individual therapy as now, but fees would have to be paid by individuals and it would be difficult to raise funds from other sources other than philanthropic individuals interested in supporting their work.
>
> Scenario B – WHC could increase its group therapy offer and adapt this to an appropriate style to fit the demands. Also, it may have to consider how it changes its position. Currently, its core offer is based on the assumption that it treats only women – this assumption may no longer be appropriate. This approach may be seen as irrelevant if the view is that the group or collective is responsible for dealing with its problems. So WHC may have to consider a radical change to include men and children, or it may consider merging with another organisation.
>
> Scenario C – WHC would be able to develop its individual therapy even further and should be able to obtain funding for its work from the health service or Social Services. The current work of WHC would be valued and seen as relevant.
>
> Scenario D – WHC would be seen as irrelevant and would cease to exist.

You can consider other fundamental assumptions about your organisation, its services and activities, and consider how these might fit into different scenarios in similar ways. The purpose of this form of planning is to stimulate thought and open discussion about situations when your organisation may face serious risk of becoming irrelevant. If nobody wants the services that you offer, or your model of service is no longer perceived as appropriate, then you will find it difficult to find funding. Also, you can think about how your stakeholders' priorities may change in a changing economic environment. If your service is seen as 'icing on the cake' then it may be dropped from the menu, as funding will be prioritised for essential services. An obvious choice for an axis on a scenario-planning grid is the length of the recession: at one extreme you assume that the recession will be short, and at the other extreme you assume that it will be long. You may wish to combine this with another axis that looks at the level of demand for your services: in other words, the needs of your beneficiaries.

Understanding the needs of your beneficiaries and their perception of your organisation is crucial at any time, but essential in an economic downturn. If you take action early enough you may be able to adapt services to meet the changed needs and ensure that your stakeholders continue to value your services.

In addition, you need to be aware of your current 'business model' – that is, the way that the demand for your services and the funding for them come together. Charities will know already that a strong demand for their service does not necessarily mean higher levels of funding. But there may be strict rules on the way that funding is used or the way that services are delivered in order to qualify for funding. The way that you run a service which is funded by voluntary donations may be very different from the way you have to run a contract with a government department or agency. Your charity may need to change the way it operates and its way of funding activities, so you need to be prepared to think through the consequences of such changes.

Managing uncertainty: using risk management in financial planning

When you prepare financial plans, you are making a large number of assumptions that need to be tested and properly understood. One way to test plans and financial forecasts is to consider the level of uncertainty inherent in them. This will help you to assess the robustness of your finances and identify trigger points when you need to take action.

Identify key drivers for costs
Typically, budgets show a summary of costs under account headings such as salaries, rent, insurance, etc. It is more useful for decision making to understand the nature of these costs and the activities that drive the costs.

Fixed costs
These are costs that are incurred regardless of activity level and are typically overhead costs and those associated with premises. For example, when you pay the insurance premium on a building you have incurred the cost and cannot reduce it, even if you decrease the activity taking place in the building. In the longer term, you would be able to reduce these fixed costs by disposing of the building. The actual amount to be paid for fixed costs can vary, just as insurance premiums can increase or decrease, but when planning, you should bear in mind that you do need to cover the whole of these costs. Organisations will usually have central costs that are effectively fixed costs – that is, the costs of managing and administering the organisation.

Variable costs

Variable costs are incurred relative to the level of activity. For example, an organisation that runs training courses using freelance trainers will be able to plan for the costs of freelance trainers by basing the estimate on the number of courses planned. Variable costs will reduce if the level of activity decreases.

To estimate the costs of an activity you need to know about both the variable and the fixed costs. Understanding the nature of the costs of an activity and an organisation can help you to see which costs will be affected by changes in demand or funding.

Case study – WHC

WHC has drawn up its budget for the year as follows:

	Total £
Income	
Counselling fees – groups	60,750
Counselling fees – individuals	20,250
Grants	65,000
Publication sales	37,957
Course fees	144,000
Café takings	225,000
Total income	**552,957**
Expenditure	
Counsellors	33,750
Course leaders	12,000
Salaries	266,850
Catering/supplies	134,205
Telephone	5,000
Postage	2,860
Printing of publications	3,000
Advertising and publicity	6,500
Stationery	2,500
Photocopying	1,000
Cleaning	1,200
Audit and professional fees	5,000
Interest on mortgage	7,500
Total expenditure	**481,365**
Surplus/deficit	**71,592**

From this budget, it does not know how much its fixed costs are, or which costs would be changed if the levels of activities change in the various areas where they operate. First, it needs to identify the different activities of the organisation:

- information service
- research
- counselling
- training courses
- café.

Second, it needs to go through the expenditure headings and identify the extent to which the costs would be incurred anyway (fixed costs), or whether the costs are incurred as a result of the activity (variable costs). For example:

- the information service employs one full-time worker (fixed cost in the short term) and incurs variable costs on phone lines
- the research service employs one full-time worker (fixed cost) and produces one report each year (variable cost)
- the counselling service is organised by WHC for which it employs an administrator (fixed cost), but the counsellors are freelance (variable cost)
- the training courses take place in its own premises, so there are no additional costs for the room, but it does provide refreshments and lunch from the café (variable cost). It uses its freelance counsellors to lead the training (variable cost)
- the café sells food and drink with a mark-up on food and beverages at about 100% on cost for prepared food, and about 30% mark-up on bought-in confectionery (all variable costs). It employs three staff (fixed cost).

Within these activities, we can see that some costs are variable, and some are fixed. So, for example, if the numbers of people using the café fall, then it would need to buy in less stock and can make savings on food and drink purchases. However, it is still employing the same number of staff in the short term. So many of the staff costs are fixed costs unless it makes a decision to close down the service.

In addition, some of the costs in the budget relate to the premises and central management and administration, which are all part of the fixed costs.

Identify assumptions underlying income estimates

To draw up a budget you have to prepare a forecast of the income that the organisation will receive. This may depend on success in fundraising, the level of take-up of users for a service or the performance that the organisation achieves if payment is linked to the delivery of key outputs. You also need to understand the relationship between income and expenditure. For example, a charity may receive funding from a grant-making trust for one of its projects, but the funding is restricted and if the charity cuts costs on the project, then some of the funding may have to be offered back to the funder.

> **Case study – identify assumptions**
>
> WHC runs training courses for professionals working in health and social service areas in the public sector as well as individuals in other charities and some private sector organisations. It runs two one-day courses per month, each with the capacity for 20 people. It charges £300 per place on each course. So income is calculated as on this basis as:
>
> $2 \times 12 \times 20 \times £300 = £144,000$.
>
> The key assumption is full capacity on each course in its income forecast.

Assess the uncertainty or sensitivity of forecasts

With a better understanding of the behaviour of costs when circumstances change, and knowledge about the assumptions underlying income forecasts, you are now in a position to consider the impact on both costs and income when you face changes in the external environment.

> **Case study – assessment of uncertainty**
>
> WHC looks at the risk associated with the training courses. The actual level of income may fall below capacity easily, so now we need to look at the relationship between income and costs.
>
> It uses its own premises for the courses, so there are no additional costs for the room, but it did have to buy furniture and equipment, which cost £3,000. It provides refreshments and lunch from the café. It uses its freelance counsellors to lead the training, which costs £500 a day including travel expenses.

It spends £3,500 on publicity and employs an administrator to run the training courses programme. Her salary is £14,000 (including employer's national insurance) for the part-time post.

The fixed costs are the salary and publicity costs, so £17,500. The amount spent on the furniture and equipment is a *sunk cost* – this is a way of expressing that it is in the past and therefore no longer affected by current or future decisions. Similarly, the costs of the premises are not included as these are incurred regardless of a decision about the training courses. Each course needs to contribute towards these fixed costs of £17,500, which is approximately £730 (£17,500 divided by 24, as there are two courses per month).

The variable costs are the course leaders' costs of £500 per course and the catering costs of £20 per head (£400 per course), so a total of £900.

Therefore, each course needs to generate a minimum of £730 to cover fixed costs and £900 to cover variable costs, so a total of £1,630. At £300 fee per attendee, it needs only six attendees to cover costs, whereas it has capacity for 20 on each course. This gives scope to reduce prices or spend more on publicity.

WHC judges this to be a fairly low-risk, break-even level. It will monitor the bookings for courses and note that it needs a minimum of six bookings at the current price.

Assessing the certainty of voluntary income

Voluntary income such as donations from individuals and funding from grant-making trusts and companies is usually more sensitive than earned income, so more prone to fluctuations and change. Different types of income will need slightly different techniques for forecasting, but it should be possible to group income into the following categories:

- confirmed
- probable
- possible
- uncertain.

Confirmed income will be when the source is known and the funds may be received already. For example, a grant or contract may have been awarded over a three-year period, so the income for future years is certain.

Probable income will describe sources such as committed and direct debit donations, subscriptions and some grants and donations where the funder has indicated that the funds will be forthcoming. You may be raising funds also through events, raffles, direct mail or applying to grant-making trusts, where your charity has experience and a track record of successful fundraising by these means.

Possible income may include new sources of funds or new funds from existing sources. It may be that the charity is trying a new form of fundraising or planning activity to recruit new members or new donors.

Uncertain income is the category of the unknown, but may include untried new fundraising methods or fundraising for which there are no detailed plans.

Once you have put different income sources and estimated amounts into categories, you can apply a percentage rate to each category to represent the degree of certainty for that income stream.

Confirmed: 100%

Probable: say 90% or 80% (due to drop-off rates as people cancel subscriptions or move away), but you should take into account activities to increase membership or regular giving

Possible 25–50% depending on your past track record in raising funds and the exact nature of the fundraising

Uncertain 0%.

You can develop your own certainty rankings for specific sources of income, and you may wish to consider very large bids to single funders separately. Once you have established the format for this, you can vary the degree of certainty to test the impact on income, in order to learn more about critical points to watch for as early warning signs.

Planning for contingencies

Once you have a framework for preparing different versions of your financial plans you can look at different scenarios to consider the consequences. For example, you can prepare several versions of the budget to show the impact of reduced levels of activity, reduced levels of income or without certain activities. You can revisit the strategic scenario planning and consider the impact on your organisation if there is significant change in the external environment in which you operate. This will give you the chance to plan and develop your ideas about contingency plans.

Reviewing your reserves policy

You may have established your reserves policy some time ago, and even if you review it annually it may be necessary to consider the policy afresh if the circumstances have changed significantly. Most charities adopt the risk identification approach, based on an understanding of the income streams and their risk profile, the degree of commitment to expenditure and the overall risk environment in which the charity operates. The steps to reviewing your reserves policy on this basis are described in more detail below.

1 Understand your funds

For this, you need to look at the charity's balance sheet and the source of funds. Some donated funds to charities may be *restricted*, which means that legally they can be spent only on the purposes for which they were given. If the charity has unspent restricted fund balances, these are not available for general expenditure and must be carried forward to be spent in the future on the specified purposes.

A charity may have endowment funds, which are the capital funds of the charity and a form of restricted fund. The capital must be retained and only the income may be spent for the purposes of the charity.

Unrestricted funds form the general funds or reserves of the charity. These are available to be spent on the charity's objects. However, the trustees may have designated some of the unrestricted funds for a particular purpose, for example the replacement of equipment. In addition, some may be effectively tied up as they have been invested in fixed assets.

Case study – WHC

Its last audited balance sheet shows that it has total funds of £214,250, made up as follows:

Restricted funds:	
– property fund	£98,000
– information and research grants	£10,500
Unrestricted funds	
– general funds	£105,750
Total funds	**£214,250**

> The property fund relates to a £100,000 grant provided in the previous year to help WHC purchase the building that it occupies. The grant is being used to fund an element of depreciation on the building and so is reducing by 2% each year.
>
> The information and research grants have been underspent in earlier years and these funds will have to be used in line with the purpose set out by the funders or offered back to the funders.
>
> Of the £105,750 of general funds, £100,000 has been used already to help purchase the property, so this is not available to WHC in the form of cash. Therefore, its liquid reserves are only £5,750. To reflect this in the balance sheet, it designates £100,000 as a property fund.

2 Review your future income streams

Start by looking at existing funding, with some assessment of the likelihood of the source of funding continuing. For example, a grant may be certain as it may be a multi-year award. For some charities, membership subscriptions will be a stable source of income, although some allowance may have to be made for non-renewals.

Other risk factors should be taken into account in assessing the funding sources. An income stream is more at risk if it comes from only one source, such as a major grant. A large number of small donations may have a lower risk profile because the chance that all donors will cease giving is very low. A few donors will cease giving, but where each donation is small, the financial impact is minimal. This can be taken into account when reviewing future income streams.

In addition, the loss of income will have a greater impact on the charity if the source of income forms a high proportion of the overall income to the charity.

A risk profile of future income streams can be built up using the following information:

(a) Type of income/source of funding
(b) Current level in £
(c) Proportion of total income as a percentage
(d) Do you expect the income level to go up or down? Rank as follows:
 1 = steady increase – by 10% or more
 2 = rapid increase – by 25% or more
 3 = static
 4 = decline

(e) How many different people give under this form of funding, that is: is this a single grant funder or many individuals? Rank as follows:
1 = very many
2 = several
3 = few
4 = one source or funder

(f) How certain is the source of income for the future? Rank as follows:
1 = committed for indefinite future
2 = for a fixed period
3 = planning well under way or by implication (for example, past pattern, verbal assurance)
4 = not certain at all.

You can multiply out the scores in the categories (c) to (f) to come to a number that will give the relative reliability of each type of income. Using the above ranking system means that a low score indicates a more reliable source of income. A high score means that there is greater risk attached to the source of income for a combination of reasons.

Using this system of ranking can help a charity to produce a table to see the relative reliability of each source or type of funding, and how secure its future income streams are. Clearly, a charity with secure income streams has less need of reserves, whereas a charity with insecure future income needs higher levels of reserves.

Case study – WHC

WHC has considered its various sources of income for reliability.

	£	Proportion of income %	Likely change	Number of sources	Certainty	Score
Counselling fees – groups	60,750	10.99	4	1	4	176
Counselling fees – individual	20,250	3.66	4	1	4	59
Grants	65,000	11.76	3	3	3	317
Publication sales	37,957	6.86	4	1	4	110
Course fees	144,000	26.04	4	1	4	417
Café takings	225,000	40.69	4	1	4	651
Total	552,957	100.00				

> This analysis shows that the size of the café takings and course fees makes these important but relatively high-risk sources of income. Another view on these activities for this calculation would be the contribution from these activities, as this is the net income to the charity. In this case, the outcome would be similar as they also generate significant net income.
>
> WHC will need to keep this information about the reliability of its income in mind as it completes the next steps.

3 Review your committed expenditure

The next step involves looking at expenditure patterns and the extent to which the charity can curtail or change the timing of cash outflows. Ideally, a charity should be timing cash outflows to match the timing of cash inflows. Where this is not possible, reserves may be needed to fund expenditure in advance of income receipts, or expenditure may need to be delayed.

You can build up a profile of the charity's commitments using the following analysis.

(a) Type of expenditure

(b) Current level in £

(c) Proportion of total expenditure as a percentage

(d) How significant is that type of expenditure to the charity's operations? How much does it contribute to the achievement of the charity's objects? Rank as follows:
1 = unnecessary
2 = optional
3 = essential
4 = core purpose

(e) Consider the number of people affected by a decision to cut expenditure, including beneficiaries, volunteers as well as staff. Rank as follows:
1 = one
2 = few
3 = several
4 = very many

(f) Identify the source of funding and score as follows:
1 = general funding
2 = grant

3 = restricted income
4 = contract.

Multiply all the scores in (c) to (f) to produce a number that may be described as the commitment score. Based on the above system of scoring, higher scores indicate a greater degree of commitment to the expenditure line.

You can decide how to split up the expenditure, but a balance needs to be achieved between too much detail and insufficient detail. The purpose of this exercise is not to identify the types of expenditure that will be cut first, but to help quantify the amount that may be needed in reserves to fund expenditure patterns.

Case study – WHC

	£	Proportion of expenditure %	Operational significance	Number of people affected	Source of funding	Commitment score
Salaries	266,850	55.44	3	3	1	499
Catering/supplies	134,205	27.88	3	3	1	251
Freelancers	45,750	9.50	4	4	1	152
Office costs	34,560	7.18	2	3	1	43
Total expenditure	**481,365**	100.00				

The salaries are a significant expense and WHC needs reliable income or sufficient reserves to ensure that these are funded.

4 Assess the level of reserves

If your charity has reliable income, then it needs a lower level of reserves. However, it may wish to create some level of reserves to maintain payments on committed expenditure in the event of a downturn in income. This would give the charity time to develop other sources of income.

If your charity is heavily dependent on a single source of funding then, arguably, it may need to hold a reserve to enable the charity to close down in an orderly fashion. In these circumstances, it is legitimate to calculate the reserves on the basis of the redundancy costs and other closure costs.

There are a number of reasons why charities may hold reserves and these will depend on the type of activity undertaken by the charity and how it operates and funds its operations. Once you have reviewed income and expenditure in an objective way, you need to consider the overall risk that the charity faces, and consider the right approach to reserves for your charity.

> **Case study – WHC**
>
> WHC needs to build reserves as its general reserves have been depleted through the purchase of the property. It needs to look at its cashflow to supplement its understanding of the risks that it faces. Income is reasonably well spread through the year, except for August, when the centre closes down, and December, when the centre is closed for two weeks for Christmas.
>
> WHC decides that it needs three months of total expenditure as a minimum reserve. This would allow it to wind down particular activities that are failing if it becomes necessary. At current levels of expenditure this amounts to approximately £120,000.

Management information

Up-to-date and relevant management information is essential for managers and trustees to enable them to steer their organisation. Speed is important here – it is better to produce prompt information about some key indicators rather than delay until all control accounts have been reconciled. This does not mean that the control activity should be ignored – it should be reconciled on a regular basis through the cycle of finance work, but it does not have to hold up the production of timely management information. In fact, the regular reconciliation of control accounts and other proper internal control measures will mean that the systems can be relied on to produce good-quality financial information at any time.

Key performance indicators

Key performance indicators (KPIs) can be identified most easily by considering the assumptions made when constructing budgets and cashflow forecasts. The cost drivers and areas of uncertainty should form the indicators that you monitor.

Indicators can provide information about how the organisation has performed, for example, the income earned from a training course. This is termed a *lag* indicator – it tells you after the event how the actual performance measured up. This will not help you to change the result of that event, but it may be helpful in planning future activities. These can be more helpful if tracked over a period of time so that you identify trends, which will form a better guide for decisions.

Lead indicators will provide earlier warning of whether things are going to plan or not, for example the number of bookings on a training course. You can use lead indicators to make short-term decisions such as cancelling a training course or increasing promotional activity.

> **Case study – WHC**
>
> WHC has identified the main risk areas as the counselling sessions (a core activity), the training courses and the café.
>
> It has decided that the KPI for the counselling sessions and training courses will be bookings, which it will track weekly. For the café, it monitors the weekly takings as a lag indicator. In fact, bookings will help it to know whether the café will be busy, as it derives most of its trade from those participating in activities in the centre.

Using management information

Regular management information to show the actual financial position should provide an overview and supplement the regular monitoring of KPIs.

One of the risks facing charities is an imbalance between restricted and unrestricted funds. For example, a charity could be quite successful at raising restricted funds, and so may have cash in the bank, but this can be used only for the restricted purposes. It may have commitments and expenditure which has to be met from general funds. It is tempting to borrow from the restricted funds cash to fund the unrestricted expenditure. However, this is not permitted and is a breach of trust, as explained elsewhere.

So, management information needs to cover three key aspects:

- restricted (project) expenditure – to ensure that projects are not overspending, as this would have to be funded from unrestricted income
- unrestricted income – to ensure that the income is being raised according to the plan
- cashflow – looking forward to ensure that the charity has sufficient funds overall.

Monitoring restricted expenditure

Restricted funds are often created as the result of an application to a government or trust fund and consist of grants to fund particular projects. Some charities have a large number of different funders and different funds supporting a range of projects and activities. It may be possible to identify the direct costs of projects fairly easily, but staff costs, overheads and central administration costs will have to be allocated to projects. Allocating costs is a detailed and time-consuming task and may not be the best use of time when prompt management information is required. One way to solve this problem is to manage costs in clearly defined cost centres. This can be done as follows.

- Project budgets should be set once the funding has been awarded to reflect the actual amount of the award rather than the bid. These should be set out to show the direct costs for each project and the contribution that the project should make towards central overheads and administration costs. The direct costs can be monitored and regular assessment made as to whether the project will make the budgeted contribution.

- Salary budgets are prepared as part of the overall budgeting exercise. The two key variables within a salary budget are the numbers of staff in post (or vacancies) and the rate of pay. Therefore, the overall staff numbers can be monitored to identify overspends and underspends. Other key changes should be picked up too, such as the use of agency or temporary staff at a different rate from the normal salary where vacant posts have to be covered.

- Central administration costs should have a budget set at the beginning of the year and a member of staff should be responsible for monitoring the expenditure against the budget. Any overspend on this central administration budget will either be allocated to all funds or may have to be absorbed by the unrestricted funds. However, the allocation does not have to be calculated for us to know if there is a problem.

Early warning signs to look out for are as follows:

- direct costs of projects running ahead of budget
- pay increases above planned levels
- staff increments running at a higher level than planned
- use of temporary staff at higher rates of pay than permanent staff
- central administration costs running at higher levels than expected, or unexpected expenditure
- underspends on some projects may also be a problem as this may mean that the project outcomes have not been delivered and that the income cannot be retained.

The risk with restricted fund projects is that the funds have been used but the terms of the funding have not been met or outputs have not been delivered. This is particularly the case with performance-related grants. (A similar risk applies to contracts, although these are unrestricted funds.) In this case, the financial accounting system may disguise a problem. On the face of it, the funding is being used to pay for legitimate expenditure, but in fact the future commitments on the project are greater than the amount of the remaining funding. This is actually an unfunded deficit and ultimately it will have to be met from unrestricted funds. If your charity has this type of restricted fund project, then it needs to ensure that reporting covers the outputs the project has to deliver. These may need to be independently verified by someone outside the project management team to ensure that the measures are being used fairly.

Restricted funds are created also when charities run an appeal for a particular purpose. If it is a substantial appeal running over a number of years to set up a fund for a new building, for example, then it may be simpler to put all the appeal funds in a separate bank account. This is much easier to manage as it does not involve allocations of costs.

Case study – WHC

WHC receives restricted funding for two activities: information and research.

Information – has one full-time worker (salary costs £25,500) funded by grants from trusts and foundations which amount to £30,000. The information service therefore contributes £4,500 to central administration costs.

Research – has one full-time worker (salary costs £25,500) funded by grants from trusts and foundations which amount to £35,000. A report is produced each year: 1,000 copies are printed, of which about 40% are given away as complimentary copies. Of the rest, about 50% are unsold. The unit cost of production is £3 and they are priced at £6.99. This information can be set out for this cost centre as follows:

Grants	35,000
Sales of report	2,097
Total income	**37,097**
Salary costs	25,500
Report printing	3,000
Total expenditure	**28,500**
Contribution	**8,597**

This shows that the grants are contributing towards the cost of producing the report. WHC needs to check that this is permitted under the terms of these restricted grants. If this is not the case, it needs to reconsider the way in which the report is produced and sold or accept that it will have to subsidise the cost of production from unrestricted funds.

Monitoring unrestricted income

Usually, the budget-setting process will identify the extent to which the charity needs to raise further funds, and the charity also may have reviewed its reserves policy and position at the same time. There may be certain expenditure and commitments that the charity has to pay from unrestricted funds. Therefore, the charity will have a target for the level of unrestricted income that it needs to generate in the year and this will need to be monitored carefully.

The timing of this income will be important, and this aspect will be picked up by reviewing the cashflow position of the charity.

Case study – WHC

WHC charges fees for a number of its activities, which generate unrestricted income. The budget had set out expectations for income from these activities, together with the associated costs and expected contribution that the activities would achieve. One of these activities is the counselling service to groups and individuals.

Income
Counselling fees – groups	60,750
Counselling fees – individuals	20,250
Total income	**81,000**

Expenditure
Counsellors	33,750
Salaries	24,000
Advertising and publicity	2,000
Total expenditure	**59,750**
Contribution	**21,250**

Assumptions

WHC runs about 30 sessions a week, but closes for five weeks in the summer (August) and for two weeks over Christmas. Each session is one hour and the rates are as follows.

Individual sessions: £40 (employed) or £10 (benefits)
Group sessions: £20 (employed) or £5 (benefits)

About 50% of sessions are for groups (six people) and about one-third of the people attending are on benefits. Counsellors are self-employed and charge £25 per session. There is a full-time organiser whose salary is £24,000 per year (including employer's national insurance).

Actual performance in first six months

Group sessions have been booking up well, but WHC is short on numbers for the individual sessions. It has had to cancel half the individual sessions, paying the counsellors an administration fee of £10 each time due to short notice.

On the group sessions, the administrator has noticed that the fees are less because more people on benefits are booking – now about two-thirds of places are allocated to people on benefits.

The administrator has calculated the effect of the trend continuing all year. This shows the effect of reduced income and reduced counsellors' fees. The administrator's salary is a fixed cost of the counselling service and the advertising has been spent already at the beginning of the year.

Income	
Counselling fees – groups	40,500
Counselling fees – individuals	10,125
Total income	**50,625**
Expenditure	
Counsellors	28,688
Salaries	24,000
Advertising and publicity	2,000
Total expenditure	**54,688**
Contribution	**–4,063**

Consequently, it will not even make a contribution towards the central administration costs, which is going to be a drain on the rest of the organisation.

WHC decides that it will have to find funding to subsidise the reduced rates on courses, or it will have to reduce the number of courses that it runs quite drastically. If it does reduce the number of courses, it will have to make the administrator redundant and cover this service from the central administration team.

Monitoring cashflow

To prepare a cashflow forecast, the charity will need to have information about the amounts owed to the charity and by the charity so that the next few months can be forecast with a reasonable degree of accuracy. A cashflow report provides information about the receipts and payments for the past few months and forecasts the receipts and payments for some months into the future. It will also show the actual bank balance at the time that it is prepared and the predicted bank balance for the future months.

A cashflow forecast that includes both restricted and unrestricted funds and all bank accounts will provide a better overview of the charity's financial position at that moment and into the future. However, appeal funds held in a separate bank account should be omitted from the cashflow forecast, as this may give a misleading impression.

You may have to think carefully about the headings used for receipts and payments in order to reflect restricted fund commitments in the cashflow forecast. It is also important to interpret the balance held in the bank correctly. While the cashflow statement may show the funds held, it can be useful to show beneath this the extent to which this represents restricted funds.

In addition, you will need to have a clear understanding about the terms on which you receive all streams of income. Traditionally, charities have been used to receiving grants quarterly in advance, however this may change to funding in arrears if you have a contract or a performance-related grant.

Case study – WHC

WHC had forecast its cashflow on the basis of its original budget. With a forecast surplus of nearly £72,000, it had hoped that it would be able to build up reserves in the year. Although it had £23,000 in the bank at the beginning of the year, only £5,750 related to unrestricted reserves.

Income is lower than expected in all activities, so now it is forecasting a deficit of approximately £100,000. This has a consequential effect on cashflow such that it is showing net cash outflows every month except April, when it receives the restricted grants for the information service. WHC will experience actual cash shortfalls in August, when it closes for the month. Even before this, it must be borrowing from the restricted grants received for the research and information services.

WHC urgently needs to change the forecast outcome, by reducing outgoings or increasing income, as this cashflow forecast shows that it cannot continue in the same way for long.

WHC cashflow forecast based on actual for six months and forecast (*continued overleaf*)

	Jan	Feb	Mar	Apr	May	Jun	Jul	Aug	Sep	Oct	Nov	Dec	Total
Income													
Counselling fees – groups	2,700	3,600	4,500	3,600	3,600	4,500	3,600	0	3,600	3,600	4,500	2,700	40,500
Counselling fees – individuals	675	900	1,125	900	900	1,125	900	0	900	900	1,125	675	10,125
Grants – information				30,000									30,000
Grants – research	17,500			10,000					7,500				35,000
Publication sales – report				583	583	583							1,748
Publication sales – book	998	998	998	998	998	998	998	998	998	998	998	998	11,970
Course fees	9,000	9,000	9,000	9,000	9,000	9,000	9,000	0	9,000	9,000	9,000	4,500	94,500
Café takings	9,000	12,000	15,000	12,000	12,000	15,000	12,000	0	12,000	12,000	15,000	9,000	135,000
Total income	**39,873**	**26,498**	**30,623**	**67,080**	**27,080**	**31,205**	**26,498**	**998**	**33,998**	**26,498**	**30,623**	**17,873**	**358,843**

Note: figures are rounded to the nearest pound

WHC cashflow forecast based on actual for six months and forecast (continued)

	Jan	Feb	Mar	Apr	May	Jun	Jul	Aug	Sep	Oct	Nov	Dec	Total
Expenditure													
Counsellors – groups	1,125	1,125	1,500	1,875	1,500	1,500	1,875	1,500	0	1,500	1,500	1,875	15,750
Counsellors – individuals	1,125	788	1,050	1,313	1,050	1,050	1,313	1,050	0	1,050	1,050	1,313	11,025
Course leaders	1,000	1,000	1,000	1,000	1,000	1,000	1,000	1,000	0	1,000	1,000	1,000	11,000
Salaries	22,238	22,238	22,238	22,238	22,238	22,238	22,238	22,238	22,238	22,238	22,238	22,238	266,850
Catering/supplies	8,435	8,435	8,435	8,435	8,435	8,435	8,435	0	8,435	8,435	8,435	8,435	92,790
Telephone	1,250			1,250			1,250			1,250			5,000
Postage	238	238	238	238	238	238	238	238	238	238	238	238	2,860
Printing of publications				3,000									3,000
Advertising and publicity	6,500												6,500
Stationery	208	208	208	208	208	208	208	208	208	208	208	208	2,500
Photocopying	83	83	83	83	83	83	83	83	83	83	83	83	1,000
Cleaning	100	100	100	100	100	100	100	100	100	100	100	100	1,200
Audit and professional fees									5,000				5,000
Repayments on loan							2,250	2,250	2,250	2,250	2,250	2,250	13,500
Total expenditure	42,303	34,215	34,853	39,740	34,853	34,853	38,990	28,668	38,553	38,353	37,103	37,740	440,225
Net inflow/outflow in month	(2,430)	(7,718)	(4,230)	27,340	(7,773)	(3,648)	(12,493)	(27,670)	(4,555)	(11,855)	(6,480)	(19,868)	
Brought forward	23,000	20,570	12,852	8,621	35,961	28,188	24,540	12,047	(15,623)	(20,179)	(32,034)	(38,515)	
Carried forward	20,570	12,852	8,621	35,961	28,188	24,540	12,047	(15,623)	(20,179)	(32,034)	(38,515)	(58,383)	

Note: figures are rounded to the nearest pound

Improving your financial position

Any charity is interested in ways of improving its financial position, but this has particular relevance if your income is at risk or potential funders are telling you that you seem to be too expensive.

In general, it is hardest to justify fixed costs and overheads, such as administration costs. It is impossible to run a sizeable organisation without incurring such costs, nonetheless it is difficult to persuade some funders that they are essential.

You may need to review your operating model if your current way of working carries high costs, although the organisation may have a strong belief in the model because of quality issues.

Review overhead costs

The first place to start is the back office costs, such as financial management, human resources (HR), information technology (IT) and premises. This may include salaries, although generally savings cannot be realised quickly on salaries. You would have to go through a proper redundancy process, including consultation, and you would have to pay notice and redundancy pay where it is due. However, in the longer term, this is often the only way to make a difference to the overall costs of the organisation.

Rather than making your own team redundant, you may be able to offer their services to other charities. Some charities have joined forces to make significant savings on HR, IT and other support activities. You may be able to take the opportunity of a resignation in a department to outsource the function to another organisation. There are commercial and charity providers of all support functions. However, you need to be clear about the specification of the service you require. It takes time and effort to get this right at the beginning but it will save difficulties later.

On premises, you may own a property or hold a lease, so the only short-term way of reducing your costs is to sub-let to another organisation and generate some income. Also, you may be able to let out meeting rooms and conference facilities if these are suitable. Or you may be coming to the end-of-lease commitments and may want to take the opportunity to move to a charity-run building or a social enterprise. There are now many such buildings, and they generally offer flexible terms so that you can scale up as you grow or reduce the space that you occupy and therefore reduce costs, if necessary.

It is generally helpful to convert costs from being fixed costs to variable costs. This enables your organisation to respond to a downturn in the level of activity or demand for your services more quickly. For example, employing staff on zero-hours contracts (whereby you only pay them when they actually work, so they are effectively on call) is a good way to ensure that you can get staff when you need them, but you are not paying staff costs when there is no work for them. This is commonly used for cover or relief staff in many charities. Similarly, sessional staff or freelancers offer flexibility and are common in training and education organisations. In some cases, you may need to offer some form of retainer or guarantee of minimum hours.

> **Case study – WHC**
>
> WHC has decided to review its position after six months of disappointing results. The forecast for the year after six months and on the assumption that things continue as they are now, shows a deficit of nearly £150,000 and a cashflow shortfall of nearly £60,000. The trustees recognise that some action has to be taken to reduce the deficit. With virtually no reserves, it has to act quickly.
>
> - It decides to stop running the café itself as this is forecast to make a deficit of nearly £20,000, although it plans to look for a provider which would run the café on a concession and pay a small rent.
>
> - It decides that additional funding is needed for the subsidised counselling places for people on benefit. If it cannot find additional sources of funding for this, it will make an administrator redundant. The period of the next three months should be used to establish a plan to reduce the cost of administrators across the organisation, in order to achieve savings of approximately £25,000. The director will be responsible for discussing with staff how this can be best achieved and further part-time working would be acceptable as an option rather than a redundancy.
>
> - It resolves to look at better ways of using the premises – possibly consolidating WHC activity to one floor and renting out the surplus space to generate some income.
>
> - It will monitor the course bookings, but wants to see further options at the next meeting to consider pricing, offers such as three places for the price of two, and further promotion.
>
> - It is still likely that there will be a deficit in this financial year, but it wants to look at the long-term implications of these proposed changes before making further cuts that would reduce its capacity to run activities which can generate a contribution.

WHC forecast income and expenditure for the year after six months actual

	Information service	Research	Counselling	Book	Training courses	Cafe	Central admin and premises	Total
Income								
Counselling fees – groups			40,500					40,500
Counselling fees – individuals			10,125					10,125
Grants	30,000	35,000						65,000
Publication sales		1,748		11,970				13,718
Course fees					94,500			94,500
Café takings						135,000		135,000
Total income	**30,000**	**36,748**	**50,625**	**11,970**	**94,500**	**135,000**		**358,843**
Expenditure								
Counsellors' fees			28,688					28,688
Course leaders					10,500			10,500
Salaries	25,500	25,500	24,000		14,000	70,200	107,650	266,850
Catering/supplies					18,000	74,790		92,790
Telephone	1,000	2,500					1,500	5,000
Postage							2,860	2,860
Printing of publications		3,000						3,000
Advertising and publicity			2,000	1,000	3,500			6,500
Stationery							2,500	2,500
Photocopying							1,000	1,000
Cleaning							1,200	1,200
Audit and professional fees							5,000	5,000
Interest on mortgage							15,000	15,000
Depreciation					1,000	10,000	10,000	21,000
Total expenditure	**26,500**	**31,000**	**54,688**	**1,000**	**47,000**	**154,990**	**146,710**	**461,888**
Surplus/deficit	**3,500**	**5,748**	**(4,063)**	**10,970**	**47,500**	**(19,990)**	**(146,710)**	**(103,045)**

EFFECTIVE FINANCIAL MANAGEMENT

Consortium bids

You may not be able to make enough savings by simply looking at overhead and administrative costs and shaving off costs where you can. For most organisations, the balance between central costs and the scale of charitable activity is the key point to monitor. If you can scale up the charitable activity, you may well get better value from your central costs.

One way to scale up charitable activity is to join other organisations in a consortium bid for funding to deliver services. This is becoming more common as more funders show a preference for dealing with one entity. You will need to decide if you are prepared to be the lead body, taking on the responsibility for delivering the services. You then will have to set up systems to pass over funds and monitor the performance of your consortium partners. For this, you should earn a management fee, so this should contribute towards the central costs.

Alternatively, you may be a consortium partner, acting as a subcontractor to the lead partner. This will enable your charity to reach more beneficiaries and access funding. In consortium arrangements you will need to ensure that roles are clear, with proper contractual arrangements, and that tax and VAT issues are handled properly.

Mergers

There are a number of good reasons to consider a merger at any time.

- Two or more charities may decide that they will be in a stronger position if they come together to bid for services. In this situation, they are likely to be providing similar services to a similar client group, but may operate in different geographical areas.

- One charity may have significant fixed assets such as property, and another may have strong service delivery. Bringing the two together will create a stronger single charity.

- One charity may have been established for a narrow cause, such as people with a specific condition. It now finds that there are fewer potential beneficiaries and wishes to apply the funds to a wider group of beneficiaries. Charity Commission permission may be necessary, but it may be possible to obtain agreement if it allows the funds to be put to good use for a similar group of beneficiaries while still caring for the remaining numbers in the original group.

- A charity with a narrow funding base may wish to diversify. A merger with another charity may achieve this, as well as offering opportunities to the second charity.

Trustees need to consider the beneficiaries first and foremost in any merger situation. They should consider whether a merger would be the best option for the beneficiaries, and not refuse a possible merger simply because it would mean staff redundancies or other change that staff would not welcome.

If a charity is experiencing financial difficulties, then the consideration of merger possibilities should not be left to the last minute. The earlier the trustees consider merger options, the better. It is easier to ensure that your charity's beneficiaries will receive the best for the future if you are able to negotiate from a position of strength. In addition, it will give a better chance to the new merged charity if it receives a healthy charity into the merger. You may wish to move only some activities or services. It might make sense to transfer an activity if it is not core to your charity but the core activity of another charity. For example, in the past few years a number of charities which had a small number of residential facilities have transferred these activities to specialist charities.

Often, mergers are perceived as a way of reducing costs, particularly overheads. To some extent this may be true if it allows the number of senior managers to be reduced, or the number of staff in central service to be reduced. However, the extent of the saving is often disappointing. In fact, the reverse may be the case, as the costs of bringing two sets of systems and two teams together can take a great deal of time and money. The actual merger process can be expensive if large charities are involved and a significant amount of external advice is required. However, smaller charities coming together can do much of this work themselves and the biggest risk is the time taken over the merger. Managers may be distracted from operational management and business development by the merger process.

So, think carefully before deciding that some form of merger may be the answer if your charity is in difficulty. However, it is likely that some charities experiencing financial difficulties will be taken over so that the service can continue to be delivered to the beneficiaries.

Cashflow management
The most urgent problem when financial difficulties begin to emerge is cashflow difficulty. Ideally, you want to match the timing of incoming cash with the timing of payments. However, some income-generating activities will require initial investment or you may need to sell on credit.

It is legitimate to take the credit period offered by suppliers, but you should ensure that you are able to make payments on time. There may be serious consequences, for example if you fail to pay rent on time to a landlord, as this often triggers their right to initiate eviction proceedings. Similarly, you are allowed to pay tax and national insurance deducted on payroll administration on the 19th of the following month. If you are unable to pay the whole amount due to delays in receiving cash, then you should call the special helpline established by HM Revenue & Customs. This also applies to VAT payments (see Further information). It is unwise to do nothing or simply hope that it will all sort itself out.

Cash collection – credit control

You must operate some form of sales ledger if you sell goods or services on credit. You need to be able to see on a daily basis who owes money to your charity. Ideally, you also need to see how old those debts are, and action should be triggered once debts go over a certain number of days. To keep this area under control, you need to be absolutely clear who is responsible for chasing debtors. This may change as a debt becomes overdue, and then very overdue. You should seriously consider the withdrawal of services if debts remain unpaid. However, before that stage, it is often more effective simply to set up a system of telephoning debtors to remind them of the payment terms. Customers are more likely to prioritise payment to your charity if you remind them regularly of the amount owed. In a downturn it is wise to collect debts promptly, as this also reduces the likelihood of bad debts.

In addition, you should consider whether you can afford credit terms. It is quite normal for the sales of publications, places on training courses and conferences to require payment in advance. If your charity is allowing credit, then customers will take it, but it may be costing you a great deal. You may need to consider revising your terms or enforcing them more rigorously.

Borrowing

Obtaining a loan or bank overdraft is certainly a valid option if you have cashflow problems. However, you need to be sure that you will have the means to repay the loan, and the lender is likely to check your cashflow forecasts very carefully. A loan will cost money – you are likely to have to pay an arrangement fee as well as interest. A loan or overdraft will *not* be an appropriate solution if the charity has structural problems, such as a shortfall in funding for a service, only if the cashflow issue is simply a matter of timing.

Conclusion

Many of the tools needed in a difficult economic environment are the same as the ones needed in any situation – good basic records and financial information that supports decision making. However, in uncertain times, you do need to be able to respond quickly to change. For that, it helps to have lower fixed costs and to operate with more of your costs as variable. You need to be confident that you have a business model that works and is well understood throughout the management team. If indicators show that underlying assumptions about how you operate are no longer valid, then you need to adapt to the new environment. Cashflow forecasting is essential and should be one of the financial management tools that you use all the time – daily, if necessary.

Glossary

Funds of a charity

Designated funds	Unrestricted funds that the trustees have earmarked for a specific purpose.
Endowment funds	A form of restricted fund that represents the capital of a charity and must be retained to generate income.
General funds	These are unrestricted funds which have not been earmarked and may be used generally to further the charity's stated objects.
Reserves	The reserves of the charity are the unrestricted funds. The liquid reserves figure excludes the unrestricted funds tied up in fixed assets.
Restricted funds	Income received where the donor has specified that the funds must be used for a specific purpose, which may be a project or a geographical area. A restricted fund also may be created by running an appeal, where the aims of the appeal determine the restriction.
Unrestricted funds	Funds to be used for the objects of the charity but at the discretion of the trustees.

Balance sheet items

Assets	The money, goods and property that an organisation possesses, including any legal rights it may have to receive money, goods, services and property from others.
Bad debt	An amount owed to your organisation that you cannot recover.
Creditors	Amounts owed by your organisation to others.

Current assets	All the short-term assets, being amounts that are immediately available or will be received by the organisation within 12 months of the balance sheet. A subtotal on the balance sheet including stock, debtors, short-term deposits, bank and cash.
Current liabilities	Amounts that are due to other organisations within one year.
Debtors	Amounts owed by others to your organisation.
Depreciation	An estimated cost that is the recognition of the wear and tear on fixed assets. It also reduces the value of fixed assets in the balance sheet.
Fixed assets	Assets held for long-term use, such as equipment. May include buildings, furniture, fitting-out, vehicles and any items that will last for more than 12 months. Also shown as 'tangible fixed assets' on published balance sheets.
Investments	Assets held to produce an income, such as shares in companies or property. Long-term investments will be classified under fixed assets, whereas short-term investments will be classified under current assets.
Liabilities	The amounts owed by an organisation.

Management information terms

Break-even	The point when the contribution equals fixed costs. When the overheads are just covered, then the organisation breaks even.
Cashflow forecast	A plan looking ahead which estimates when income will be received and payments made.
Contribution	The contribution is the net income of an activity resulting from the deduction of variable costs from the income.
Fixed costs	Fixed costs relate to the infrastructure and central administration of an organisation and are incurred even if the level of activity reduces.
Key Performance Indicator (KPI)	This is a measure relating to an objective which provides useful management information about whether the objective is being achieved.
Lag indicator	A measure that provides information after an activity about the performance.

Lead indicator	Gives early warning as to whether the objective is likely to be achieved, as it will be a measure of one of the underlying drivers of performance.
Performance-related grants	A form of grant funding that specifies certain activities to be completed to qualify for funding.
Variable costs	Variable costs are costs that vary in direct relationship to the level of activity and therefore have a constant relationship to the income for the activity. If you cease the activity, the variable costs will no longer be incurred.

2 Fundraising in an unpredictable market

Introduction

We predict unpredictability! During a recession the one thing we can be sure of is that we will be fundraising in an unpredictable market. When economists today look at the 1990s recession they can describe a fairly neat pattern of 18 months of economic downturn and falling consumer confidence, followed by 18 months of recovery. At the time, that pattern was not discernable until we were firmly into the upward trend.

Fundraising during the last recession actually did not follow such a neat pattern. At the worst moments of decline there were sudden opportunities, such as massive reductions in the use of direct mail resulting in a temporary uplift in responsiveness as the public received fewer mailings. At the points of greatest recovery there were sudden dips in giving, such as donors who had given faithfully throughout the dark times deciding that they could ease back on their support because the charity would be all right.

In an unpredictable market it is important to monitor the market, perhaps through the press, economists and emerging research, to understand what is happening. However, do not forget that media hype is not the reality of your donors' lives. After an initial period of concern, donors generally settle down until reality bites them directly, for example in the form of reduced income, employment uncertainty or rising household expenditure. The point at which the media lose interest and move on to more interesting stories may be the precise point at which the recession is affecting your donors badly. Your priority is to see behind the media hype to understand the reality of what is happening in your supporters' lives. Practise 'donor obsession' – tune in to their values, their thoughts and their lives.

This chapter looks at different ways in which you can use the opportunities in a recession to build a rapid response team, focus on your core activities and the more profitable fundraising activities, and emerge a fitter fundraising operation as the economy emerges from recession.

Learning from the past

During the recessions in the 1980s and 1990s, fundraisers had few reference points to look back at what would help them to learn from the past. One of our strengths today is that we have a wealth of quite recent experience to draw on because it is fewer than 20 years since the last recession. Many of our most experienced current practitioners have fundraised through one, if not two, previous recessions. Our fundraising programmes have developed in the past two decades, but there are still substantial similarities, and one of our great strengths in 2009 is that we can reach back quite easily and bring forward lessons that will help to guide our strategy today.

The corporate sector learns from the past, reflects actively on the present and continues to paint scenarios for the future. This is a healthy mix that we should seek to replicate in the not-for-profit sector. With our comparatively limited resources, and our relatively young profession, we should not be afraid to look at the actions taken by companies that are surviving and thriving in the current climate and ask ourselves what learning we can take from their actions. The key is to accept the situation and to drive forward in an informed way. You cannot simply close your eyes and hope things will not change – they will, as you can see on any high street in the UK today.

Looking to the future

New tools
We have a number of new tools in our armoury this time round. Three in particular stand out.

Regular giving
First, we have the well-established monthly direct debit-based regular giving programmes that are the backbone of our individual giving programmes today. Direct debits have a dramatically positive impact on retention. In the last recession we did not have these at our disposal, we were almost entirely dependent on cash giving. So those organisations which have invested strongly in regular giving programmes are entering this recession in a much stronger position this time around.

Digital media
Second, we have digital media. In the early 1990s, the internet as we know it simply did not exist. Email was largely a tool for communicating inside your organisation. Mobile phones were the size of a modest handbag and weighed as much as a brick. This low-cost, low-risk, mass-contact medium is far from being exploited fully, and offers us a communications channel that will be sustainable throughout the recession.

Donor journey

Third, we have spent the past decade redefining and reinforcing the 'donor journey' – the different stages that an organisation presents to a donor to embrace, increase and enhance their relationship with a charity. Depending on how far you have developed this area, you are likely to have a valuable and well-defined group of high-value and major donors – core individuals with the capacity to invest more in your cause. Like everyone else, this group may feel uncertain about the economic environment, but they represent a core donor group which has a sufficiently strong relationship with you to continue investing, and perhaps to invest even more, during these challenging times. Even if some need to slow down with their pledges, do not slow down with your cultivation and relationship building: this will ensure that their intention to give is not lost and that their gifts will be forthcoming as the market stabilises.

> Charities should consider the impact of the recession on the need and on beneficiaries. The NSPCC knows that child abuse is more prevalent when people are financially stretched, and therefore we need our donors to give more rather than less in times of recession.
>
> Every organisation should engage its donors with its problems; tell your donors just how serious the situation is and how urgent the need for money. The NSPCC emergency appeal in early 2009 raised £1 million in cash, and has hopefully persuaded a lot of people who might have been thinking about cancelling their direct debits to keep supporting us.
>
> Charities need to hold their nerve. Recessions are awful, but they do come to an end. Do not be afraid of running a deficit for a year or two; reserves exist for precisely this situation, to help you to survive during difficult times.
>
> Giles Pegram, Director of Fundraising, NSPCC 1979–2009

Embrace change

In an unpredictable market, your attitude and response to change will determine your organisation's success as much as, or perhaps more than, any other factor. Take the right opening stance and you can survive (even thrive) in a downturn.

At the start of a downturn the focus is inevitably on worsening conditions, downward trends, and the need to protect the organisation from damage and loss. A defensive strategy may seem logical, and indeed by cutting back your investment you may avoid short-term losses and minimise your risks. However, if you maintain this defensive stance in the medium and longer term it will be counterproductive, leading you to miss opportunities and be poorly placed to take advantage of the market upswing when it eventually occurs.

When the recession hit fundraising in the 1990s it was a little like falling off a cliff. We had no real idea of how far down the bottom was, how long it would take to get there, indeed whether we would ever be able to climb back to the top. Some chose to sit still, avoid anything risky and wait until we hit bottom. Some kept on doing what they knew, and what they had always done. After the first shock had worn off, others turned themselves into a rapid response team: this meant tuning themselves into the market more fully than before, making sure that they were ready to defend or take risks, to evaluate situations and make fast decisions, to act quickly or stop suddenly. It was this last group which ultimately weathered the recession best of all because they were best placed to find the crucial balance between protecting their assets and seizing sudden opportunities.

The faster you accept that you are in an unpredictable market, the faster you can start driving towards it as opposed to reversing away. Difficult times call for confident action. You will be able to assess and respond to the marketplace faster than the competition who have stopped or are busy reversing. Be prepared with 'insurance tactics' to try to pre-empt negative changes in donor behaviour.

Be intelligent

'Tuning in' means systematically monitoring the market to understand how the events happening now are likely to impact on your fundraising. Think about the direct impacts (positive and negative) on individual donors, such as their employment status, inflation, the cost of utilities, petrol and food, interest rates for mortgages and savings income. Think also about the more emotional impacts around consumer confidence, and an individual's belief that it would be better to save their money or just wait and see what happens before spending or giving.

Tune in to what your competitors are doing, especially those that are in the public eye or that your donors are likely to know. The behaviour of these kinds of charities can affect your donors as much as your own behaviour, and you need to be ready to respond. For example, once a major charity plays its 'emergency shortfall' card this sends a significant message to donors, and you need to be clear whether the most appropriate response for you is to follow suit or to reassure your donors that you are not in that position.

Watch carefully, too, for opportunities arising from changes in other charities' behaviour. For example, the withdrawal of major charities from one form of fundraising may leave the field free for your organisation to do more, or for you to negotiate better rates with a key supplier who may need to fill capacity urgently.

Some charities have difficulties in obtaining fast, accurate performance results. If you are to be effective as a rapid response team you must be able to assess results quickly. Experience in the last recession showed that small opportunities opened up for short periods, and it was only the swift who could exploit them fully before the market changed again. If your analysis is several months behind, the opportunity may have come and gone before you knew it was there. This is crucial for the market upswing stage. You need to have your finger on the pulse in real time, otherwise other organisations will be off and running ahead of you. The flip side of this, of course, is that if you are not closely monitoring performance you may continue to invest in a form of fundraising for many months after it has become unviable. An important area to watch closely is early attrition rates on those recruitment channels which are already fairly marginal for lifetime return on investment.

> It is important to not let yourself be unnerved by what you read or hear during a recession, or to become over-cautious. When the Red Cross held a major appeal for Kurdish refugees during the last recession, many people said it was too risky and that donors would not give, but in fact it was so successful that it provided the launch platform for today's Red Cross donor programme.
>
> If you have a good cause, and a good appeal, people will still want to give. Even if they can't give right now, keep talking and building relationships. For those corporate and major donors who are hard hit now, don't delay making an approach, but think about asking for a pledge for a future gift, or suggest that giving is spread across a number of years. Stay confident.
>
> John Gray, Director of Advocacy, Action for Children 1981–1989; Director of Communications and Fundraising, British Red Cross Society 1991–2001

Nurture your fundraising expertise

In a recession you will need to call as never before on your fundraising expertise. Every day your 'rapid response' fundraising team will need to respond, decide and innovate. Every fundraising programme you have will need to be made to work harder. Every donor you have will need to be communicated with more intensely and more persuasively.

Your fundraising team is the driver of your fundraising, and if you reduce your investment in expertise you reduce your capacity to drive your fundraising forward. In a recession you need to drive as hard as you can just to stand still. To reduce your fundraising expertise in a recession is therefore a deliberate decision to reduce your income.

Organisations that went the route of reduced investment in their fundraising teams in the 1990s learned this the hard way. Yet as early as autumn 2008, in many cases before any impact of the recession had been felt, organisations were agreeing staff reductions and recruitment freezes across the board. Clearly, it is important to be fair and transparent in these situations, but it is equally important to recognise that expert fundraisers are an investment for the whole organisation. Retain your fundraising resource at full strength and you will have the best chance of maximising income, which in turn will mean that other staff members have the best chance of retaining their posts.

This is particularly important for programmes where income is raised very directly by fundraisers, for example major and corporate gifts, and grant applications. Quite simply, without this resource, the income will vanish, because it will not have been asked for in the first place. Mass cash appeals are also a key area that require proactive asks to be made.

In an unpredictable market you should consider increasing your investment in staff training, team-building and developing the right culture for success in your charity. When the media bombard people with economic messages of doom and gloom it is unsettling for people in any profession, so fundraisers need to hear, see and feel strong support from the trustees and directors of their charity. Now, more than ever, people need to grow their skills and stay completely up-to-date with market developments and opportunities. Redundancies in any part of the organisation will send shock waves that will unsettle staff across the board, so building a strong team that it is supported by the organisation, and where team members support each other, is crucial to carrying key staff through difficult times.

Challenging as it may be, difficult times can be a good time to recruit, as good fundraisers are made redundant, choose to leave unsettled teams or look around for new challenges if their own resources are being cut back drastically. The UK is suffering from a shortage of skilled fundraisers, a trend that is likely to continue well after the current market challenges begin to fade, so take any opportunity you can to bring good people on board if they become available. They are your strongest investment for future success and growth, even if this means a financial stretch in the short term.

Also, consider also your external fundraising expertise. Your fundraising programme is likely to be dependent on a range of consultants, designers, copywriters, data analysts, production specialists, recruitment and telephone teams, as well as freelancers who supplement your in-house resource. It is in your own interest not to act in such a way that you cut yourself off from this source of expertise, even if this seems attractive in the short term. A good fundraising team will always need external specialists; it simply does not make sense to have every skill needed in-house.

Stand out from the crowd

During the recession you are likely to be competing with the same number of charities that you were before, and some of those charities may be seeking more money if their work increases during a time of greater social and economic need. At the same time, the number of donors who are active may decrease: they may give to fewer charities and the amount of their giving may be reduced. Therefore, the market is likely to be even more competitive, and it will be even more important for your organisation to stand out from the crowd.

Make your message easier to understand, talk to your donors in language that they understand, not your internal 'mission speak'. Make your message more resonant – tap into the current concerns of your donors, show them that you understand their situation and do not make them feel guilty about not being able to give as much. Be clear, bold and persuasive about your case for support. Why should people support your cause when times are hard or uncertain and it would be safer to sit on their money for a while longer? Why should people keep supporting *your* organisation if they have to make a choice between several?

In this digital age, there are more than 200 channels you can use to reach out to and communicate with your donors. Even before the current economic crisis it was becoming increasingly critical to refresh and shift your channel mix on a regular basis, but in this climate you can use your choice of channels genuinely to stand out from the crowd. You may be able even to dominate a particular communications channel at some point in the year, thus providing an automatic advantage. During March, Comic Relief dominates the television and the cause-related marketing channels; in May, Christian Aid dominates the house-to-house collections channel.

During the last recession charities such as the NSPCC were able to drive hard at the market with a 'low monthly ask' proposition: £2 a month. This was clearly good value in the eyes of the donor and seemed to be a good way of continuing to give in difficult economic times. This developed a very strong, committed giving base of donors who became the foundation of NSPCC success and income today. Already we are seeing charities revisiting techniques such as low monthly ask propositions on the basis of continuing to recruit donors in a difficult marketplace. Standing out from the crowd is not always about doing new things; it can be about doing simple things well, with confidence and passion.

Managing your portfolio

Focus on your core business
Fundraisers have a well-established practice of 'jumping on the bandwagon' of new ideas. In a predictable, growing market there are many such opportunities and temptations to expand your fundraising, and to achieve a modest level of success. For

more than a decade we have been fundraising in a market which has fostered this type of expansion and many charities today have very diverse portfolios indeed.

It is important, of course, to have a degree of diversity to spread risk, especially in an unpredictable market. However, there is a point at which the diversity of your portfolio becomes a risk in itself. You may be stretching your resources too thinly. You may have too many marginal activities, which quickly could become loss-making during a downturn. You may be investing too much of your fundraising expertise in new areas where you make only a small amount of net income, to the detriment of your major established income streams.

In an unpredictable market, the highest risks are related to the areas of your business which are furthest away from your 'heartland'. For example, the donors for whom you are fifth choice, the donors who have been with you the shortest time, the fundraising techniques where you have the least expertise. The last recession taught us that it is our core business that is most likely to weather the recession, and that this is where we should be focusing our investment. Your portfolio should be diverse, but within the context of core business.

First and foremost, your core audience is the people who already support you and have supported you for a minimum of two years. When looking to recruit new supporters, you should focus on the people who care most about your cause and your organisation. They are most likely to support you through hard times if you are a high priority for them, if you are part of their donor 'A' list.

Evaluate your fundraising programmes. Your core programmes are those that generate the largest amounts of net income and general funds. They are the programmes you are very good at, where you can offer something special and outperform everyone else.

Now is the time to invest in stewardship at every level of your operations so that you have the highest chance of not only continuing to hold on to your donors, but also of building their loyalty, so that their relationship with you is even stronger on emerging from the current recession. Think of the potential of taking a 360-degree view of your supporters: money, time, gifts-in-kind, voice, influence and lifestyle change to align with your mission. Too much focus is given to monetary support, and in hard times it is the other areas of support which can help to retain and inspire your donor. The more ways a donor engages with your cause, the stronger their support at all levels. Be empathetic to what they may have to cope with in their lives as a result of the unpredictable market. Difficult as it is with ever-pressing financial targets, it is better to allow a donor to give time or engage in campaigns rather than lose them altogether by continually pushing for donations that they simply may not be able to give.

> My advice is to cut out non-essentials, for example the more experimental areas of your fundraising which have a higher risk of losing money. Focus on the areas that work and that really earn money.
>
> In particular, look after your existing donors, prioritise retention over recruitment. Make the most of mechanisms such as direct debit – the RSPB was ahead of the game with the introduction of direct debits to its membership, and as a result it was able to retain a higher proportion of its members than other organisations during previous recessions.
>
> Think long-term about investing in legacy marketing; what really matters is achieving continued growth in the number of notifications. The housing market will eventually recover, and if you have increased notifications you will be well placed to see your income grow beyond its earlier peak.
>
> Anthony Clay, Head of Fundraising, RSPB 1979–1988

Prune selectively but vigorously

As every business knows, at the end of the day there are only two core strategies: make money or save money. After two decades of unprecedented growth, it is inevitable that many charities will have built up areas of resources that 'tick along' but frankly are not necessarily core to the fundraising activities. The process of defining your core business will identify these less viable or more marginal areas of your fundraising programme that need to be pruned.

Pruning always should be selective, and there are different levels of pruning depending on the current and future prognosis for each fundraising area. A light pruning may be appropriate for a fundraising programme that is modestly profitable, low-risk, needs little resource to maintain it and has potential for growth when the market recovers. A moderate to strong pruning may be appropriate for a fundraising programme that is not profitable at present, but is expected to recover in more favourable conditions – you may decide to maintain this programme at a minimum level of investment.

Some fundraising programmes may need to be closed down. They may be seriously loss-making, and cannot be maintained with an acceptable minimum of investment or have no obvious potential for recovery. Or they may be loss-making programmes which can be restarted quickly when the market recovers.

Alongside your pruning, consider also a 'replanting' approach, where you move resources from areas of low yield to those of high yield. It is always difficult to move people around, especially as we tend to have structures based increasingly on specialists, but if head counts are frozen or the challenge is simply to work with what you have, replanting resources to reinforce areas with the greatest potential may help you to gain the forward momentum you need. For example, you might consider moving some of your corporate fundraisers into major donor fundraising if corporate income is particularly vulnerable, but major donor fundraising is still delivering.

Sustainable income streams

One of the greatest lessons of the last recession was the collapse of ad hoc giving compared to committed giving. In the 1990s, direct debit giving was not widespread and most giving was cash. Cash-committed giving such as membership survived the recession in reasonably good shape, but giving by ad hoc donors was affected badly. Many uncommitted donors simply paused their giving. For the donor this was a pause, often restarting when the market recovered, but the impact on the charity was a total loss of its income, in many cases for several years.

From this it is clear that you should be prioritising income streams that are based on *commitment*, because these income streams are more likely to be sustainable during the recession. These include the obvious income streams such as regular giving via direct debit, but there are many other forms of commitment, including regular cash giving, multi-year pledges and contracts. Again, do not be afraid to ask donors for deferred giving if this is a way of maintaining their commitment – the same amount of support but phased differently.

General fund

Make sure you understand your general fund needs. It is often the case that committed giving and general fund go hand-in-hand, but not always. General fund is crucial for the stability of the organisation, for paying your overheads and often for enabling you to accept major grants that do not cover their overheads. General fund gives you flexibility, fuels investment and enables you to be fleet of foot. Ultimately, it allows you to maintain your organisation even if you have to reduce your direct expenditure for a period of time. Make sure your fundraising is generating sufficient net general funds for your survival – if necessary, accept less income: for example, a donor who would give you £200,000 earmarked might give you only £100,000 for general fund, but this could be more valuable for your organisation at this time.

Seek dialogues with donors to explain the importance of general funds, especially in difficult times. Where major donors are still giving they may be more sympathetic to a request for a percentage of general funds built into what otherwise would be a restricted grant. Foundations always have been tolerant of the need for a general fund percentage in their grants, but this requires transparency and an upfront ask.

Raising consciousness of the types of funding generated by different programmes is the starting point for protecting this area. Over the boom times of the last decade we have seen a dramatic increase in restricted funds programmes, as they are often high value or volume, and now is the time to review your strategic approach.

> It is the size of your net profit that matters, not the size of your gross income or supporter file. Don't be afraid to plan to let your supporter numbers decrease if this will help you to maintain or grow long-term net income. Build and strengthen the commitment of the supporters you already have, keeping and upgrading them is much more important than recruiting new supporters.
>
> During the 1990s recession, WWF-UK 'strategically reduced' our supporter numbers by 10%. We were prepared to take a one-off hit on the cost of recruitment during the recession, provided that we were investing in potential long-term committed supporters. We spent most of our time and resources on improving the quality of our fundraising and on increasing the value of giving of every supporter we had. Despite the smaller file we ended the recession with 20% more net income, and a new high in the quality of our fundraising programme – which gave us the springboard for the next five years of exceptional growth.
>
> With your cash donors, it's important to rethink the meaning of 'lapsed'. Expect your cash giving to be hardest hit, but view donors who stop giving as 'pausing' rather than lapsing. Work hard to continue to nurture your relationship with them, to make sure that the pause will be followed by renewed giving. Locate your 'super-donors' – the people for whom you are the number one cause – and ask them to increase their support for a limited period, to help you through these hard times until other donors pick up their giving again. Our experience at WWF was that these super-donors found the opportunity to make a real extra difference enormously rewarding, and it increased their feeling of closeness to the organisation long term.
>
> Margaret Bennett, Head of Individual Giving and Director of Fundraising, WWF-UK 1988–1997

Fundraising strategy

Prioritise profit over growth

Big is not always beautiful. 'Doubling gross income in five years' is not the only fundraising strategy. Indeed, gross income should not be the focus of your fundraising strategy at all. Usually, the investment required to drive gross income growth – especially where recruitment is initially loss-making – will reduce your net income in the short to medium term.

Net income is the amount that is available to the rest of the organisation to spend on the mission and organisational overheads; maintaining net income should be the goal during a recession.

The last recession followed a period of significant growth from the late 1980s onwards, so charities with professional fundraising expertise were focused very strongly on large-scale recruitment of new supporters and growth on a major scale. The impact of the recession was most severe on the ability of charities to recruit new supporters, especially less-committed supporters. Growth was halted abruptly, and in many cases reversed, as charities were unable to recruit enough new members to replace attrition.

An important lesson learned from this was that, despite the decline in gross income, some charities were able to maintain and increase net income by refocusing on the retention and development of core supporters. So do not be afraid to plan a decrease in gross income or number of supporters, if this will lead to a sustainable increase in net income.

Donor development

Put your greatest effort into keeping the supporters you have already. Develop the relationships you have with them, and aim to increase their giving. From the commercial world of marketing we know that it costs five times as much to recruit a new customer as it does to keep one you already have, and existing customers will spend up to ten times as much with you as new customers. This applies equally to donors.

Switch from the 'recruitment' mindset to the development mindset. Start by refocusing your investment: as rule of thumb, work out how much it costs to recruit a new supporter and set that as the maximum that you can spend on retention.

Focus on those areas of donor development that will keep your donor supporting you throughout the recession, bearing in mind that a key way to grow net income is to keep more of your supporters. Maximise direct debit and other committed giving schemes that will lock donors in more tightly. Review the information and reporting to your donors to be sure that they are getting what they are interested in, when they want it. Offer your supporters a choice of communication channels to meet their preferences. Consider the range of other engagement opportunities for donors that will bring them closer to the organisation and encourage them to stay. Put in place a 'supporter journey' to engage supporters in the way they want to engage, and to maximise lifetime value for your organisation.

Identify options for increasing the average amount of giving per supporter. Gift Aid should be top of your list as it costs the donor nothing. Continue to increase average giving, but be targeted and sensitive. Encourage your donors to consolidate their charitable giving with your organisation by demonstrating how you will spend their money most effectively.

America entered the current recession several months before the UK and there are some useful lessons that should be explored. In particular, the re-emergence of 'member-get-member' or 'donor-get-donor'. This is a well established, and in many ways old, marketing philosophy which has not worked particularly well for many charities over recent years, but in times when people simply cannot give any more, it can be another way for them to help their favourite charity. Instead of trying to upgrade donors at the normal time, think about asking a donor to introduce a new donor – true 'people power'. There is a lot of emphasis in our sector on integrating with social networking sites, but while we explore this route let us not forget the traditional ways of moving into communities, groups of friends and networks generally – good old word of mouth.

Invest and test

Fundraising teams need to work closely with their financial colleagues to get agreement as to why it is dangerous and short term to cut investment in fundraising programmes. A charity needs to explore every other option before taking investment away from the one area which can help it to navigate out of an unpredictable market, as well as protecting the future security and growth of a charity and its vision for those it serves.

When you have identified your core business, and you are tuned in to the market and your donors, invest strongly. Investment is essential for protecting your current programmes and donors, and to refresh and strengthen your offers so that you stand out from the crowd and compete effectively. You also need to invest to make sure that you are ready to take immediate advantage of every opportunity and manage every risk. Being tuned in to the market means continuing to invest in donor, market and competitor research, as well as allowing time for fundraisers to network. It also means investing in a different kind of fundraising test programme. In a normal market, the expectation from testing is that it will be viable and subsequently can be developed into a larger programme; there would be no point testing something known to be unviable. However, in a recession, a number of viable programmes or techniques may become temporarily unviable but be expected to recover following a market upturn. In these cases, it is the market that is being tested through a rolling low-level programme that monitors performance with a view to identifying the point of market upturn and the point at which the fundraising programme becomes viable once more. Once this is established, investment can be increased.

Instead of continuing to pursue the same strategies as last year, charities need to take a completely fresh look at what the market is doing and decide on a different creative, marketing and promotion mix. It should be highly targeted and concentrated. Being flexible, up-to-the-minute with information, in control and brave are the key qualities needed to continue to invest in recruitment of committed givers in the current marketplace. A charity should never stop testing or investing unless it is truly forced to do so – these are the lifeblood of a successful programme.

> Cards for Good Causes' turnover went up by a considerable amount during the last recession. Our experience was that the public was even more determined that any money they were donating would go to a good cause; the 'Cards for Good Causes' brand communicated this message loudly and clearly.
>
> My advice for charities in this recession would be to review, and if necessary change, your message to ensure that it gets across the 'good cause' and demonstrates how you can make donors' money go further. If you can communicate this effectively, then rather than reducing investment, now is the time to invest as much of your resources as you can, to take advantage of the opportunities that the recession will bring to raise even more money than before.
>
> Judith Rich, Director, Cards for Good Causes 1976–2000

Innovate

Focusing on your core business does not mean sticking with what you have done in the past. Indeed, innovation is crucial in a recession.

If the experience of the last recession is repeated, innovation in recruitment will be a major challenge. Where organisations are dependent on cash gifts, the need for innovation perhaps will be greatest. Can you develop appeals and funding opportunities that capture the imagination of your donors to such an extent that they give despite their own financial anxieties?

Digital fundraising is a potential area for innovation, being low investment and with the potential to generate a high volume of recruits or contacts. Despite many years of discussing digital fundraising there is still only a small proportion of charities fully harnessing the potential of digital media and social networking. This is an area of incredibly rapid change, with new opportunities opening up every month, yet many charities are still debating banner advertising as an option when it should by now be commonplace.

The quality of online recruits is very high in terms of average gift and attrition rates, the latter at least partly because of the element of 'self-choice'. Online donors (such as direct marketing donors) are making an independent, conscious decision to give, as opposed to being stopped in the street and 'talked into it'.

Linking into the 'development, not recruitment' focus, online relationships have the double attraction of being exceptionally low cost and, with investment in the right technology, almost infinitely customisable. Digital media is finally providing us with the ability to give every single donor a personally customised relationship with our charity. What better way to ensure the retention of your donors than to be able to treat each one as an individual, even if you have millions of donors?

Partnerships with companies and grantmakers

Effect of the recession on corporate partnerships

Traditionally, the most active corporate sectors for charitable support are the financial, construction and retail sectors, so inevitably corporate fundraising is extremely difficult in an unpredictable marketplace on the scale of the one we are now facing. The challenge is obvious: in a market where the City is crumbling, consumer spending is uncertain and the housing market is in decline, companies have to take immediate action to compensate for the economic environment, and this includes curtailing, delaying or cancelling charity links and partnerships.

Charities are reporting advanced discussions being closed down, partnerships being cut short and an overall reluctance to open up new discussions. On the surface, this may lead to the conclusion that corporate fundraising should be suspended, but this would be short-term thinking, would not recognise the progress made in the past decade and would not ensure a balanced portfolio for the future.

It is interesting to look at what our American cousins are doing, as they are at least six months ahead of us in terms of recession, and there are some interesting case studies of how partnerships and cause-related marketing programmes are holding up. Pure charitable giving largely has dried up, unless it is through the corporate foundation; however, community programmes continue to survive (although not necessarily thrive), and the general dialogue between charities and companies in trying to bring about change in corporate practice continues apace.

There is a natural synergy between the not-for-profit and the corporate sectors, and we have more than 25 years of dialogue and partnerships in place that have shaped a well-tuned and proven portfolio of techniques, partnerships and case studies. The challenge now is to reshape our thinking and approaches. Corporate marketing teams are going to be more demanding, expecting every activity to deliver on multiple fronts.

Charities with a strong corporate portfolio or a track record need to hold firm and implement a new strategy to get through the next two years successfully. They need to prepare to emerge stronger and in a new shape for the future. Charities new to this area should look much harder at their cause and brand, and ask themselves whether they should revise expectations and scrutinise resource commitments in a very unpredictable market.

Most experienced corporate fundraisers realise that often the least important part of a corporate partnership is money; the focus needs to be on a corporate partner as a 'route to market'. It is the operations and outreach of a company which offer the most attractive opportunity for a charity brand, whether that is to their customers, consumers or the general supply chain that the company sits within and influences. Corporate fundraisers need to invest more in research to understand supply chains and enable them to have more informed dialogues with companies, showing how they can unlock support from a wide range of other stakeholders.

Deeper corporate alignment

For years we have overused the word 'partnership' dramatically in trying to secure links and support from companies. This always has felt comfortable for all parties, although by now, many companies experienced in this area are quite cynical about the term, knowing that charities rarely deliver a true partnership.

Charities need to move beyond identifying a link between themselves and a particular company and go much deeper into the logic of any partnership, primarily driven by the brand. Are there shared values between the company and the charity? Do you share goals or visions in the same areas, for example around climate change, human rights or wanting to focus on cancer care in the UK? Does your structure or regional coverage match the company's in some way? (This is critical in retail, where they may want direct links to staff or volunteers.)

Now is the time for charities to think about their campaign, advocacy or education messages. How could specific companies help you to deliver these messages by reaching out to their customers, consumers and suppliers? Companies tend to welcome these types of proposition, as they enhance their brand qualities, can be a real added value to their propositions and build a link with a charity that is anchored more genuinely in shared values and objectives.

At an even deeper level, you can work with a company to bring about changes in the way that they conduct their core business. This can cover a wide range of areas, from working with the HR department on HIV in the workplace, through to labour rights and procurement policies. Companies welcome this form of engagement when the market is unpredictable as it can help them to 'get their house in order' during a difficult period, often enhances their reputation and can form an important part of their 'licence to operate'.

Companies themselves recognise that the most valuable things they can do to contribute to charitable causes are centred on changing the way that they do business and recognising the power of sharing their communication channels. In many ways, corporate fundraising should be developed across the whole charity, thinking through the power and impact that it can have in contributing to the vision of the charity, rather than simply another income channel.

> On Monday 19 October 1987 the world experienced the largest one-day percentage decline in stock market history. It became known as 'Black Monday' and it took several years for the economy to recover. Eight days later, HRH The Prince of Wales launched the Wishing Well Appeal for the Great Ormond Street Children's Hospital.
>
> So, did this financial disaster dash our hopes? To be honest, we never contemplated failure, in spite of the economic crash that month, because this was the most emotive of causes, backed by an enormous engine of specialist volunteers who had helped to orchestrate mass public coverage for the appeal.
>
> A major sophisticated marketing campaign was in place, promoting a drip-feed of televised and high-impact key events all over the country, backed by parents who owed the hospital so much – in many cases the lives of their children. When the appeal was in full swing it was bringing in £2 million a month. Altogether, £84 million was raised for the appeal (including £30 million negotiated from government). That equates to about £150 million in today's money.
>
> I think this proves that, even in the face of a major financial recession, if your cause is compelling and emotive, and enough people care about the outcome, you can still pull off a major fundraising campaign. But making a strong case takes great care to ensure that you can really justify your plans and that they stand up to rigorous scrutiny from the major potential donors who must be convinced.
>
> Otherwise, during recessionary times, I believe charities should concentrate on having enough funds to maintain their existing services to their beneficiaries and use the time to build their infrastructure and cultivate new and existing relationships, ready for better times.
>
> Marion Allford, Director, the Wishing Well Appeal for Great Ormond Street Children's Hospital 1985–1989

Trusts and grant fundraising

The key in this area is to plan for a 'delayed effect': the money being distributed in grants now was the interest trusts gained on their investments 12 to 18 months ago. As we move further into the recession, the true impact of the market will affect the funds that grant givers have available to distribute.

In early 2009, the general view of grant givers is that they will continue to give, but they will need to limit the number of new initiatives and dialogues, and focus on those charities where they already have commitments or relationships. Consequently, it will be difficult in the next two to three years to make approaches from cold as the funds available will shrink. In the same way as we advise charities to focus on their existing donors, grant givers may do likewise with their existing partners.

Increase the amount of communication that you have with existing grant supporters; try to understand the challenges and circumstances that they are facing; and share with them how your charity is progressing. Strengthen your research to track and understand what is happening in the grant-giving market, as things will change quickly, with short-term opportunities potentially arising.

Do not be complacent – you will need to deliver even more in terms of reporting and accountability, because grant givers are likely to look for greater value from every investment. They will need to demonstrate that they are maintaining their impact despite a lower level of funding, and despite their inability to take on new partners.

Conclusion

Is the recession an opportunity to invest in the future of fundraising? To end on a positive note, the last recession also made fundraisers much smarter. To survive, we had to be more tuned in, respond faster, innovate more and build better, stronger relationships with our donors. We came out of the recession with stronger fundraising programmes, and it was these programmes that laid the groundwork for the quality and quantity of fundraising that we have today.

If history repeats itself, then in two or three years we could be looking at another big step up for the professionalism of our fundraising. We hope that this will include a major transformation in the extent to which fundraising through digital media and social networking is a mainstream programme. If we emerge from this recession with a win such as this, we will be able to look back on it as not just a short-term problem, but also as a time of investment in the longer-term growth of our fundraising capabilities.

3 Legal aspects to managing in a downturn

Introduction

A downturn inevitably forces the trustees and executives of charities to consider whether or not their charity will be able to weather the storm. Therefore, it is vital that you understand the legal framework that governs your organisation, charitable or not. Inevitably, the 'i' word – insolvency – is used frequently.

The effect of insolvency on different legal structures

Charities operate under a great variety of constitutional forms. These include companies limited by guarantee or by shares, societies incorporated by Royal Charter, industrial and provident societies, unincorporated associations or trusts and, soon, the charitable incorporated organisation. The law relating to insolvency affects charities differently depending on how a charity is constituted. If a company is incorporated, the Insolvency Act 1986 will apply. This Act also applies to a limited extent to industrial and provident societies as set out in the Industrial and Provident Societies Act 1965. Royal Charter bodies are covered by the Insolvency Act 1986 under the provisions relating to unregistered companies.

However, only a small proportion of all registered charities are set up as limited companies, industrial and provident societies or Royal Charter bodies. The majority of charities are unincorporated as trusts or unincorporated associations. Where unincorporated charities become insolvent, the liabilities pass to the trustees and the bankruptcy laws (which apply to individuals) will apply if the trustees are unable to meet the liabilities of the charity out of their own personal assets.

It is possible, under the Charities Act 1993, to incorporate a body of trustees, allowing them to execute documents in the name of the charity and be sued under its name. However, this form of incorporation does not limit the liability of the trustees. If an incorporated body of trustees faces insolvency, then the trustees will be personally liable just as if the trust were not incorporated.

Consequently, the impact of insolvency varies depending on the way in which the charity is constituted. That said, however, the tests for insolvency set out in the Insolvency Act 1986 which apply to limited liability companies, industrial and provident societies and Royal Charter bodies, also apply to unincorporated associations or trusts.

The tests for insolvency

There are two tests for insolvency under the Insolvency Act:

- the going concern test
- the balance sheet test.

The going concern test

The basis of this test is whether the company can pay its debts as they fall due. It is also known as the cashflow test. In technical terms, it is applied in various cases.

- For the purposes of a declaration of solvency (a prerequisite for the solvent winding up of a company), the directors have to state whether the company will be able to pay its debts in full, plus interest, over a 12-month period.

- Section 123(1)(e) of the Insolvency Act 1986 provides that a company may be wound up by order of the court as insolvent if it is unable to pay its debts as they fall due.

Most businesses go bust, not because they run out of work but because they run out of cash. Therefore the cashflow test is vital. In particular, the attitude of the organisation's bank is key. If a charity has an overdraft facility and the bank is happy for it to be utilised, then that could enable the charity to continue trading. The cash available through the overdraft allows the charity to continue its activities, while waiting for monies due from debtors or funders. If the bank decides to withdraw the overdraft facility, however, then the charity may not be able to pay its creditors. Effectively, the charity has run out of cash, even though it may still be solvent on the balance sheet test (see overleaf). That will be scant comfort if there is no money to pay the bills.

In the decision of *Re Cheyne Finance plc (In Receivership)* (2007) EWHC 2402, Mr Justice Briggs considered how one should view debts falling due in the future, the timing of cash flows and the ability to use funds to pay certain debts. The implication of the case seems to be that not only should directors of a company consider whether the company can pay its debts now as they fall due, but also whether it will be able to pay its debts in the future. Mr Justice Briggs stated:

> *Cashflow or commercial insolvency is not to be ascertained by a slavish focus only on debts due as at the relevant date. Such a blinkered review will, in some cases, fail to see that a momentary inability to pay is only the result of a temporary lack of liquidity soon to be remedied, and in other cases, fail to see that due to an endemic shortage of working capital a company is on any commercial view insolvent, even though it may continue to pay its debts for the next few days, weeks or even months before an inevitable failure.*

Mr Justice Briggs gave the following example:

> *The company has £1,000 ready cash and a very valuable but very illiquid asset worth £250,000 which cannot be sold for two years. It has present debts of £500 but a future debt of £100,000 due in six months. On any commercial view the company clearly cannot pay its debts as they fall due, but it is or would be, balance sheet solvent.*

The balance sheet test

Under this test, insolvency denotes the actual or anticipated deficiency of assets available to meet the company's liabilities. This is set out in section 123(2) of the Insolvency Act 1986, which provides a second reason for winding up a company. If the value of the company's assets is less than the amount of its liabilities, including its contingent and prospective liabilities, the company is technically insolvent. Again, of course, directors can use this test not just at the point of insolvency, but as an ongoing test to check the viability of the organisation.

The balance sheet test has some major limitations. First, many balance sheets do not reflect the actual financial position of a company when there may be doubt about its going concern status. For example, tangible fixed assets are stated usually at cost, but this does not tell you about their market value. Similarly, equipment may be depreciated on a straight-line basis over a period of years, but its actual market value may be much less than its depreciated value as shown in the accounts.

Second, some charities follow different income and expenditure recognition policies and this will have an impact on the balance sheet. For example, some charities may recognise a debtor for future grant income while others may not; some recognise future grant commitments while others do not.

In addition, contingent liabilities are often by their very nature difficult to ascertain. Frequently, annual financial statements will not disclose some major contingent liabilities, for example those arising under a lease of a building for dilapidations, or the risk that a lease which has been assigned might come back to haunt the assignor if the new tenant fails to meet its obligations under the lease. This is because it is assumed that these liabilities will be met as they fall due under the going concern basis.

However, the major problem with the balance sheet test is the inter-relationship with the going concern test of calculating liabilities. Under the going concern test, it is assumed that a company will continue to trade and, therefore, that liabilities which would crystallise should the company cease to trade are not taken into account in assessing its actual or contingent liabilities. The going concern test is rather like a bicycle. So long as the cyclist maintains forward momentum, all is well. But if the rider loses impetus, the bicycle wobbles and falls over. Crash! So too with a company.

If the calculation of its assets and liabilities is made on the basis of the company ceasing to trade ('break-up' basis), rather than on the going concern basis, the effect on the company's balance sheet is likely to be dramatic. First, the value of its assets may have to be written down – secondhand goods almost certainly will command a much lower price on the open market than their book value as stated in the balance sheet.

Second, ceasing trading will cause a number of major liabilities to appear and thus inflate the company's indebtedness. For example:

- staff will be made redundant, thus triggering compensation payments for notice periods and redundancy
- under the Pensions Act 1998, insolvency will trigger a discontinuance event and a requirement to pay up immediately any deficit in the pension fund
- leasing companies which have hired out photocopiers, computers, cars or other equipment may terminate their contracts and demand all future instalments due under the terms of the lease, less a small discount to reflect early repayment
- the landlord of leasehold premises will demand any overdue rent and potentially terminate the lease and demand dilapidations
- claims may arise for breach of contract to deliver services
- professional charges will be incurred to handle the winding-up of the charity or transfer of its activities
- grants may have to be repaid, as a large number of grant terms and conditions contain an obligation to repay grants should the recipient go into insolvent liquidation.

Hence, if the balance sheet test is calculated using the break-up basis, almost inevitably the results will be much worse.

In a sense, the going concern test and the balance sheet test work hand-in-hand. So long as the company can pay its debts as they fall due, the directors are entitled to calculate their assets and liabilities using the going concern test. However, as soon as the company is unable to pay its debts as they fall due, the balance sheet test should be calculated on a break-up basis – the effect of this would be to show almost certainly that the company fails both the going concern and balance sheet tests.

The question of the going concern basis is covered in the Financial Reporting and Auditing Standards. Consequently, whenever a charity prepares accounts which have to give a true and fair view, accounting standards are vital.

Financial Reporting Standard 18 Accounting Policies

Financial Reporting Standard 18 states:

21. An entity should prepare its financial statements on a going concern basis, unless:

    - the entity is being liquidated or has ceased trading; or

    - the directors either intend to liquidate the entity or to cease trading, or have no realistic alternative but to do so, in which circumstances the entity should prepare its financial statements on a basis other than that of a going concern.

22. The information provided by financial statements is usually most relevant if prepared on the hypothesis that the entity is to continue in operational existence for the foreseeable future. This hypothesis is commonly referred to as the going concern assumption. Financial statements are usually prepared on the basis that the reporting entity is a going concern because measures based on break up values tend not to be relevant to users seeking to assess the entity's cash-generation ability and financial adaptability.

23. When preparing financial statements, directors should assess whether there are significant doubts about an entity's ability to continue as a going concern.

24. If the directors, when making the assessment required by paragraph 23, are aware of material uncertainties related to events or conditions that may cause significant doubt upon the entity's ability to continue as a going concern, paragraph 61 requires them to disclose those uncertainties. In making their assessment, the directors should take into account all available information about the foreseeable future.

25. The degree of consideration necessary to make the assessment required by paragraph 23 depends on the facts in each case. When an entity has a history of profitable operations, which are expected to continue, and ready access to financial resources, detailed analysis may not be necessary. In other cases, the directors may, in making their assessment, need to consider a wide range of factors surrounding current and expected profitability, debt repayment schedules and potential sources of replacement financing. Such considerations also govern the length of time in respect of which this assessment should be made.

Obviously, one of the most difficult questions to resolve in assessing the impact of the obligations under the Financial Reporting Standards is what is meant by the 'foreseeable future'. Some believe that this is restricted to one year from the date of approving financial statements, but in fact, it is better to consider this as a minimum period, and if there is a foreseeable event in a later period it would need to be taken into account. This certainly ties in with the judgment in *Re Cheyne Finance plc* (see page 51).

Auditing Standard on going concern
The Auditing Standard on the going concern test explains that:

It is not possible to specify a minimum length for this period: it is recognised in any case that any such period will be artificial and arbitrary since, in reality, there is no 'cut-off point' after which there should be a sudden change in the approach adopted by those charged with governance. The length of the period is likely to depend upon such factors as:

- *the entity's reporting and budgeting systems; and*
- *the nature of the entity, including its size or complexity.*

The implications for different legal structures

The insolvency of limited companies
The debts of a limited company are its alone. If a company is insolvent, the limited company may be forced into insolvent liquidation. The directors of that company will not incur any personal liability for the debts of the company except in limited circumstances involving fraud, wrongful trading or breach of trust (covered later in this chapter).

The insolvency of trusts
The position is very different for a trust, and also for unincorporated associations. In either case, there is no separate entity with limited liability because the trust or unincorporated organisation has no legal personality of its own. The debts of an unincorporated organisation are ultimately the responsibility of the charity trustees out of their own personal assets.

This is made very clear by the fact that if a trust is sued for a debt, it is the charity trustees' names that will appear on the claim. If a trust incurs an obligation, for example it enters into a lease, it is the charity trustees' names that appear on the lease. As already mentioned, the Charities Act 1993 does allow charity trustees to incorporate the trustee body, but this does not affect the charity trustees' personal liabilities, as the charity itself remains unincorporated.

Indemnity clauses
Many trust deeds and constitutions for unincorporated organisations contain an indemnity from the organisation to the trustees for any liability properly incurred by them in the course of fulfilling their duties as trustees. Many people naively think that this indemnity is sufficient protection for them against the risks of being a trustee. However, of course, the indemnity is only as good as the strength of the charity's balance sheet. If the charity is insolvent, the indemnity is worth nothing – not even the paper on which it is written. For example, a charitable school run through an

unincorporated trust ran into financial difficulties. The school had to be closed and the teachers were made redundant. There were insufficient funds in the school's reserves to meet the redundancies, so the governors (that is, the charity trustees) were taken to court and had to settle the outstanding redundancy costs out of their own personal assets to the tune of £5,000 each. The indemnity in the trust deed was useless.

Joint and several liability

For unincorporated charities, the liabilities of trustees for the debts of the charity are 'joint and several'. What this means is that all the trustees could be held equally liable (that is, jointly), or that the whole or a large part of the claim could be pursued against any one of the trustees (that is, severally). If the liabilities of the trust exceed the trustees' personal assets, the charity trustees themselves could be forced into personal bankruptcy.

A creditor may petition for the bankruptcy of an individual if that person owes an amount above a minimum of £750 and appears to be unable to pay or to have no reasonable prospect of being able to pay. This position is established if they have been served with a statutory demand and since then have neither complied with the demand, nor applied to have it set aside. A creditor can decide to sue only one of the body of trustees, picking the person that they think is most likely to pay (that is, the trustee with the most assets). The charity trustee who unfortunately has been 'picked off' in this way has the right to petition the court for a contribution from each of the other trustees for a proportionate part of the debt due. Under the Civil Liability (Contribution) Act 1978 the court has the power to award in favour of one trustee against another a contribution of such amount as the court considers to be just and equitable, having regard to the extent of the responsibility of that other trustee for the loss. Also, the court may exempt any person from liability to make a contribution.

Trustees can protect themselves in contracts by stipulating that the liability of the charity's trustees is to be limited to the assets of the charity, effectively meaning that trustees incur no liability at all. While this may be possible for negotiated service contracts, it is difficult to amend standard form contracts such as those that come with hired equipment. Under employment law, it is not possible to include such a limitation in contracts of employment. In addition, this does not limit the trustees' liability in relation to other suppliers or people with whom the charity has dealings, but no contracts.

Trustee indemnity insurance

To cover this and other risks it is possible to take out trustee indemnity insurance; however, note that such insurance does not underwrite charity trustees' liabilities for the debts of a charity due to a third party if the charity is insolvent, any criminal act or where the trustee has acted deliberately or recklessly. Therefore, it is neither a financial guarantee nor a protection against trading risks. That said, such policies generally cover the personal liability arising from breach of duty, breach of trust, negligent performance of duties, error or omission, or wrongful trading. Since February 2007 it has been possible for trustee indemnity insurance to be purchased by the charity for the benefit of its trustees, provided the charity's constitution does not expressly prohibit such a purchase (section 73F of the Charities Act 1993).

It is important to remember that new trustees must take steps to remedy any breach of trust that they discover on becoming a trustee or they may become liable for that breach of trust, even though they were not trustees at the time that the breach was incurred. Trustees continue to remain liable for any breaches of trust committed during their term of office, so even if the charity becomes insolvent after that trustee has resigned, if that person was a trustee when the breach was incurred, they may be held liable.

The insolvency of unincorporated associations

The members of the management committee of an unincorporated association are in the same position as the trustees of a charitable trust – they too are charity trustees – with the possible difference that they also may be liable as members. Under the rules of an unincorporated association, the members of the association, who elect the management committee, may agree to indemnify the management committee for the liabilities properly incurred by them in serving on the management committee. It must be emphasised that the management committee can make the general members of the association personally liable for the debts of the organisation only if the constitution clearly gives them that power, or if the members sanction the liability within the constitution.

In such circumstances, if an unincorporated association is unable to pay its debts as they fall due or if its liabilities exceed its assets, ultimately the members of the association may be liable equally for the association's debts. However, a creditor will be entitled to sue the members of the management committee, who will be deemed to have been responsible for the running of the association. The members of the management committee will have to seek their indemnity from the members if this is appropriate: that is, if the constitution allows it. As you may appreciate, pursuing a large number of members of an unincorporated association for their equal contribution to the debts of the association can be difficult and expensive.

The insolvency of organisations with limited liability

The position with these organisations compared to unincorporated organisations in the case of insolvency is stark. By and large, the magic of limited liability means that the debts of the limited liability organisation are its alone. Charitable companies normally are limited by guarantee, which means the members will be liable only for the amount of their guarantee, usually a nominal sum of £1. The liability of past and present members of an industrial and provident society to contribute for the payment of debts and liabilities is qualified by special provisions under the Industrial and Provident Society Act 1965. The trustees do not have personal liability: they can sleep safe at night without concern that their personal assets may be used to discharge the debts of the organisation. There are certain exceptions to this rule, as set out below.

Fraudulent trading

Under section 213 of the Insolvency Act 1986, the court, on the application of a liquidator, may declare that any persons who were knowingly parties to the carrying on of the business with the intent to defraud creditors of the company or for any fraudulent purpose may be made liable to make such contribution to the company's assets as the court thinks proper. The intent to defraud creditors must be proved and the onus of proof is on the liquidator. There must be evidence of actual dishonesty.

It should be noted that it is not only the directors who could be made liable for fraudulent trading in connection with an insolvent charitable company. In addition to the charity trustees, the employees could be made liable for fraudulent trading (if proven). For example:

Re Grantham (1984) QB675 – it was held that an intent to defraud might be inferred if the person concerned obtained credit when he knew that there was no good reason for thinking that funds would be available to pay the debt when it became due or shortly afterwards.

Re A Company No. 001418 (1988) BCC526 – a company went into insolvent liquidation owing £212,681. The court held on the facts that there had been fraudulent trading. It ruled that a person was knowingly party to the business of the company having been carried on with the intent to defraud creditors if:

- at the time when debts were incurred by the company he had no good reason for thinking that funds would be available to pay those debts when they became due or shortly afterwards

- there was dishonesty involving real moral blame according to current notions of fair trading.

The chairman, managing director and the major shareholders had to pay £156,000 to the creditors.

Wrongful trading

This was introduced by section 214 of the Insolvency Act 1986. It was designed to counter criticisms that fraudulent trading was too difficult to prove and creditors were suffering due to the negligence of directors, but the negligence fell short of fraud.

Wrongful trading is designed to cover cases where the persons concerned have failed to exercise sufficient diligence in monitoring the company's affairs and in taking corrective action when insolvency loomed, but where they have not acted in bad faith or fraudulently.

Wrongful trading applies both to directors and shadow directors of companies registered under the Companies Acts. It also applies to directors of industrial and provident societies and bodies incorporated by Royal Charter. For the purposes of the Companies Acts, a director is anyone who occupies the position of a director, whatever they are called. It is not necessary for the director to have been registered as such at Companies House. Hence, this could include a chief executive who is accustomed to running the organisation. A shadow director is a person in accordance with whose directions or instructions the directors of the company have been accustomed to act. This does not apply where the directors act on advice given to them by that person in a professional capacity. In the case of a charitable company, it is possible that a charismatic and powerful chief executive (who is not a trustee) could be treated as a shadow director.

Wrongful trading is established if the court concludes that at some time before the company went into insolvent liquidation a person who is or has been a director or shadow director *knew or ought to have concluded* that there was no reasonable prospect that the company would avoid going into insolvent liquidation. A defence would be that the court is satisfied that the director(s) took every step with a view to minimising the potential loss to the company's creditors that they ought to have taken. Note that the fact that a company is trading while insolvent does not necessarily mean that the trading is wrongful, as long as there is a reasonable prospect of it not going into insolvent liquidation. Neither is it wrongful trading where, as Buckley J said in *Re White and Osmond (Parkstone) Ltd* (1960) (unreported), the directors 'genuinely believe that the clouds will roll away and the sunshine of prosperity will shine upon them again and dispense the fog of their depression'. This has become known as the 'sunshine test'. Therefore, there is nothing to prevent directors incurring credit to help them get over the bad time, but section 214 of the Insolvency Act 1986 does impose on directors the risk that trading while insolvent may lead to personal liability.

The test for wrongful trading is an objective one. The director must act as a reasonably diligent person, having both a director's knowledge, skills and experience, and the general knowledge, skills and experience which *reasonably* may be expected of a person carrying out the same functions as the director. The standard expected will vary from one case to another. In *Re Produce Marketing Consortium Limited* (1989) BCC569 the judge held that the expertise expected of a director is much less extensive in a small company in a modest way of business with simple accounting procedures and equipment than in a large company with sophisticated procedures.

This is of particular relevance to charity trustees. The trustees of charitable companies are almost invariably non-executive directors. They meet infrequently, say four to six times a year, and will be very dependent on the professional paid staff. They have to trust their staff. This is entirely fair and reasonable. In *Norman v. Theodore Goddard* (1991) BCLC1028, it was shown that a director is entitled to trust persons in a position of responsibility until there is a reason to distrust them.

The crucial question is: what standard of care will the court expect of a charity trustee in a wrongful trading case? There has been no case on this point to date. Will it be a lower standard than that of a full-time employee who is also a director? We consider that it would be reasonable to argue for a lower standard of care for a charity trustee who is a volunteer compared to a full-time paid employed director. However, it must be emphasised that a person with financial or legal skills or a financial function (for example, the treasurer) would be judged on the basis of these skills and thus be at greater risk than other trustees.

Under section 1157 of the Companies Act 2006, the court has the power in any proceedings for 'negligence, default, breach of duty or breach of trust' against any officer of a company to wholly or partly relieve that person of liability as it thinks fit, if the director has acted honestly and reasonably and if, having regard to all the circumstances, they ought fairly to be excused from liability. However, it has been held that this section does not apply to wrongful trading. In other words, if a director is found to be guilty of wrongful trading, they cannot look to section 1157 to be exonerated from liability. In addition, the court may make a disqualification order against a director under the Company Directors Disqualification Act 1986, which can be for a period of up to 15 years. Acting as a trustee while disqualified is also an offence under section 73 of the Charities Act 1993.

Breach of trust

If a charity becomes insolvent and creditors are unpaid, there is a good chance that there will be adverse publicity in the press or a complaint will be made to a member of parliament or to the Charity Commission. In each case, this could trigger an inquiry by the Charity Commission into the conduct of the charity's affairs.

If the Charity Commission's inquiry concludes that the charity trustees have been negligent in the conduct of the charity's affairs, the Charity Commission has the power to petition the High Court for an order that the trustees make a contribution from their own personal assets to the charity to compensate it for the loss suffered as a result of the breach of trust by the trustees. Negligence can constitute a breach of trust. It also has the power under section 15 of the Charities Act 1993 to appoint a manager who will act for the Charity Commission in respect of the property and affairs of the charity.

This can apply to any charity however constituted, whether incorporated as a company or unincorporated. Limited liability gives the charity trustees no protection in these circumstances.

In practice, such orders against trustees are rare. It is possible for a trustee to apply to the court or the Charity Commission for relief from liability for breach of trust. For such relief to be granted the Charity Commission would have to be satisfied that the trustee had acted honestly and reasonably and ought fairly to be excused for the breach of trust or duty (section 73D of the Charities Act 1993). Relief can be full or partial.

Looming insolvency: the practical implications

If insolvency looms for a charity, the best course of action for the trustees will vary according to the organisation's constitutional structure.

Unincorporated charities

On the one hand, as the trustees are personally liable in an unincorporated organisation, if the charity is facing financial difficulties, the trustees' primary aim will be to minimise the build-up of liabilities and to raise cash. If attempts to generate income or cash fail, then in view of their personal risk, the trustees may be keen to run down the organisation or seek a merger so as to minimise the chance of their incurring personal debts or even bankruptcy as a result of the charity's insolvency. Trustees in such a position should be aware of any potential conflict of interest which may arise between their concerns for their own personal liability and their duties as trustees to act in the best interests of the charity.

On the other hand, closing down will cause new liabilities to crystallise, and it is easier said than done. Many charities will have long-term liabilities, for example a lease on a building (which it may prove impossible to assign). The landlord may hold them to the lease, extracting the rent from the trustees personally. The trustees then may find themselves obliged to continue to pay rent and service charges, even after the charity has ceased to operate. Hence the need to monitor the charity's financial position and meet regularly, even for companies (see below), applies equally to unincorporated charities.

Companies

In the case of a limited company, the charity trustees will be anxious to ensure that the protections of limited liability are not lost: this means avoiding any allegation that the charity trustees have been guilty of wrongful trading or breach of trust.

Charity trustees must be able to show that they have taken all reasonable steps to minimise the loss to the company's creditors. This has the following consequences.

- The trustees have to recognise that their primary duty is no longer to fulfil the objects of the charity, but to act in the best interests of the creditors. Hence, they should aim not to incur further liabilities or expend money on charitable purposes, but instead endeavour to pay off the creditors. It may seem inappropriate for a charity to refuse to pay, for example, a grant to a beneficiary, and instead use the funds to pay the leasing charges for a photocopier. However, once they are aware of the potential insolvency of the charity, the duty to act in the best interests of the creditors – even if that means failing to act in the interests of the beneficiaries – is paramount.

- There is a real dilemma facing charity trustees in such circumstances. They must be neither cowardly nor rash. They must neither rush into liquidation (which might damage the interests of the creditors), nor must they plough on with careless disregard of the potential damage to creditors. They must not be carried away by the idea that because the charity fulfils a noble cause, this allows them to ignore their legal obligations to creditors. Neither should trustees succumb to the inherent optimism of many that, in the words of Mr Micawber, 'something will turn up'. To protect the charity trustees from a claim of wrongful trading, their actions must have been reasonable as viewed from the standpoint of a reasonable director. Belief in the possibility of trusting in providence (cynical though this may sound) is not likely to be regarded by a sceptical judge as being reasonable.

- The trustees must ensure that they have taken appropriate written legal and financial advice to show that they have acted responsibly. Such advice should be given to all the trustees. It is not sufficient for it to be given to the chair or chief executive. Trustees should ensure that advice is passed on to all the trustees, so that together they can make an informed decision. Equally, the adviser should try and ensure that this is done.

- The trustees should hold prompt and regular meetings to show that they have taken matters seriously and acted with the interests of the creditors in mind. This may mean – if time is short – that charity trustees have to meet at the weekend and must meet more regularly than at normal times. Trustees monitoring their financial position carefully will meet weekly, if only by telephone.

- The trustees should ensure that proper and detailed minutes are kept of all meetings so that there is an adequate paper trail to show how and why decisions were reached. Provided that decisions are made carefully and with the benefit of professional advice (assuming, of course, that the charity has the financial resources to pay for it), a court will be reluctant to substitute with the benefit of hindsight its own commercial judgment for that of the charity trustees, unless it considers that no reasonable director could have concluded that the act taken was in the interests of the charity.

Treatment of endowment and restricted funds

Permanent endowment

Section 96(3) of the Charities Act 1993 states that:

a charity shall be deemed to have a permanent endowment unless all the property held for the purposes of the charity may be expended for those purposes without distinction between capital and income.

The crucial question in the case of an insolvency is whether or not permanent endowment property is available to discharge the debts of the charity. The answer to this question will depend on how the permanent endowment property is held.

In the case of a limited company, it cannot hold permanent endowment property absolutely. Instead, it holds it as trustee of a separate charitable trust. Consequently, if the company goes into liquidation, the assets of the trust are not available to discharge the general debts of the company because those assets do not form part of the company's general property. If the company is wound up, then a new trustee will have to be put in its place by the Charity Commission, exercising its powers under section 16 of the Charities Act 1993. This applies to Royal Charter bodies and industrial and provident societies, which are also corporate bodies.

If the permanent endowment is held by an unincorporated trust and is not held in a separate legally constituted trust, then it is considered that the permanent endowment will form part of the assets of the unincorporated trust and be available in calculating the assets of the trust to offset against its liabilities.

Expendable endowment

Expendable endowment is not permanent endowment and, therefore, the analysis of permanent endowment and its effect on an insolvency does not apply to expendable endowment. However, it is possible that expendable endowment may constitute a special trust, depending on how it has been established, so care must be taken in this regard.

Restricted funds

How restricted funds held by a charity are treated in an insolvency is a difficult question. In guidance published by the Charity Commission, *CC12 – Managing Financial Difficulties and Insolvencies in Charities*, it states at paragraph 34:

it is a breach of trust to use restricted funds for purposes other than those for which they were given.

This very sweeping statement needs analysis. Whether or not restricted funds form or do not form part of the charity's general assets depends on the terms upon which the charity has received those restricted funds. Company law recognises that if a company receives monies, for example magazine subscriptions where the subscriber pays in advance to receive 12 copies of a magazine in a year and the subscription is put into a separate trust account, then the trust account is not available for the liquidator to use to help pay off the company's general debts, should the company go into insolvent liquidation. Rather, the surplus in the subscription account is held on trust for the subscribers. If, on the other hand, the subscriptions have just been paid into the general bank account of a company, they would have been spent and lost and the subscribers would just have a claim as an unsecured creditor alongside everyone else.

Is the position different in charity law? It depends on the degree to which the provider of the funds has required the recipient charity to recognise that the restrictions imposed on the use of the monies are a distinct and separate trust from the general trust created in charity law. Is it a 'special trust'? A special trust is defined in section 97(1) of the Charities Act 1993 as:

> *property which is held and administered by or on behalf of a charity for any special purposes of the charity, and is so held and administered on separate trusts relating only to that property, but a special trust shall not, by itself, constitute a charity for the purposes of Part VI of this Act.*

Part VI relates to separate reporting and preparation of accounts for charities and so does not specifically cover the relevant issues here of whether the funds would be available to pay off creditors in an insolvent liquidation. However, the Charity Commission gives examples of special trusts, including:

- funds related to a school to provide prizes or bursaries

- a fund belonging to a charity that advances a religion to help fund the maintenance of its place of worship

- a fund donated to a charity for the general relief of the poor to provide an income to be used to help special beneficiaries, such as the elderly.

However, what is the position of a charity which has a series of different funding streams from, for example, different government departments where it receives grant funding to support different projects? Is each of those separate grant agreements a special trust? Because if they are, any unspent funds would not be available to meet the liabilities of the charity, but would be restricted and could be spent only in fulfilment of that trust. This is a vital question that affects many charities. In reality, because of the pressures of cashflow and the slowness of some grant funders to pay, many charities rob Peter to pay Paul. In other words, they receive grant funding for Project A and pay the money into the charity's general bank account. They are also promised money for Project B and are under pressure to start on Project B, but the cash has not arrived yet. They have sufficient cash from Project A to start Project B, so they start Project B. Provided that the funds for Project B come in, the fact that they have 'raided' Project A money to kick-start Project B is not a problem. However, is it a problem if the charity goes into insolvent liquidation? Will a shortage in the funds of Project A (due to the subsidy to Project B) mean that the trustees have been in breach of trust? If they have, then this is potentially very serious for the trustees, because they could be held to be personally liable for a breach of trust and thereby be liable to repay the amount of misspent money. If that is the case, then the protections of limited liability will be of no use whatsoever, because limited liability is not a protection against a breach of trust.

Therefore, determining whether or not a restricted fund constitutes a special trust is absolutely vital. Surprisingly, there have been no cases on this issue, although there may be in the years to come. For a special trust to be created it is vital that the donor makes it clear in the grant that they expect the monies to be treated as trust monies. Consequently, the funder should stipulate that the grant be held in a separate bank account marked 'Trust Account', and drip-fed to the charity's general bank account to meet liabilities incurred solely in relation to that project. If that is the set-up then this certainly would constitute a special trust. However, very few grant funders specify this. If a funder has acted in this way, it would be consistent with the judgment in *Knight v. Knight* (1840) 3 Beav 171, a landmark case in English equity law which sets out the test to determine whether a trust has been validly constituted. Lord Langdale MR formulated the test known as the three certainties. This test specified that, for a valid trust, there must be certainty of:

- intention (there must be intention to create a trust)
- subject matter (the assets constituting the trust fund must be readily determinable)
- objects (the people to whom the trustees are to owe a duty must be readily determinable – this latter point is less important in charity law where the Attorney General or the Charity Commission can exercise this power).

In addition, for charitable trusts, the trust must be exclusively charitable.

The crucial issue here is certainty of intention. The language used by the donor must be imperative and without ambiguity. Most grant terms and conditions do not display sufficient certainty of intention to create a special trust.

Designated funds

Designated funds are funds which have been designated by the trustees for a particular purpose, and therefore can be 'de-designated'. Consequently, designated funds will be generally available for the trustees to discharge the charity's liabilities and will be accessible by creditors.

Managing your way through a possible insolvency crisis

First, review your legal structure. If insolvency is looming and you are carrying on activities through an unincorporated charity, is there any possibility of trying to address some of the risks by transferring the assets and liabilities of the charity to an organisation with the protections of limited liability? This would involve setting up a company limited by guarantee at Companies House with the same objects as the unincorporated organisation, then registering it at the Charity Commission. From April 2010 (at the earliest) unincorporated organisations will be able to apply directly to the Charity Commission to become charitable incorporated organisations, an incorporated structure regulated solely by the Charity Commission. Once the new charity has been registered, it would be necessary to execute a deed of transfer, transferring all the assets and liabilities of the old unincorporated charity to the new incorporated charity. How successful this would be, should the new charity then go into insolvent liquidation subsequently, is a moot point. At that point the creditors of the charity might seek to pursue the individual trustees on the basis that prior to the transfer of the assets and liabilities to the new charity, those creditors would have had a claim against the trustees personally, because they were not protected by limited liability.

Under company law, a preference can be set aside if it takes place within two years if it involves an associated or connected party. Clearly, the new charity would be a connected party to the old charity, but this reorganisation would not be subject to those provisions. If the trustees could show that at the point that they made the transfer the charity was capable of paying its debts as they fell due on the going concern basis, taking into account foreseeable future liabilities, then they should be safe from potential personal liability. If, on the other hand, it could be established that at the time that the transfer was made it was clear that the unincorporated charity was unable to pay its debts as they fell due, bearing in mind foreseeable future liabilities, then the position would be different. Consequently, the moral of this point is that, if you are going to reorganise your affairs, it is vital to seek the protection of limited liability and to do it quickly and swiftly while the charity is still trading solvently on the going concern basis. Another option is to look for a merger partner or organisation to take over the potentially insolvent one. However, charities should be aware that there are generally a number of obstacles to overcome when merging, such as transferring property such as leases and permanent endowments, and employee benefits such as pensions.

If you are worried that your charity may be facing cash flow difficulties, then rule number one is not to ignore it. The ostrich position – head in the sand – is not a sensible approach. Face up to the problem early. Get as much data and information as you can, as quickly as possible. Make sure that the numbers you are looking at are correct. Challenge assumptions about income. Query whether or not debts are really recoverable. Analyse expenditure and make sure that you really understand the charity's financial position. It is amazing how often, when faced with a financial crisis, trustees find that the base data that they are relying on is not reliable.

Obviously, there are two key ways of dealing with a cash flow crisis:

- increase cash
- reduce expenditure.

The crucial legal issues in relation to these possible steps are set out below.

Increase cash

This can be done in a number of ways. The best and simplest way is to get supporters to give money in a tax-efficient way to the charity, but this may not be possible. However, it may be possible to obtain a loan from a bank, or a supportive institution such as the Charities Aid Foundation's Venturesome Fund, or supporters. Lenders in these circumstances almost certainly will want to take security for their loans. Obviously, this will prompt further questions.

Can the charity borrow funds?

Surprisingly, the trust deeds or constitutions of some charities are silent on this matter. Even though there is an implied power to borrow, it is probably best to have an express one. Remember, if you are securing a loan by mortgaging your property, you must comply with sections 38 and 39 of the Charities Act 2006.

Are there existing creditors with the benefit of security?

If so, then you almost certainly will have to get their consent to borrow further funds. They almost certainly will demand a 'deed of priorities' to ensure that the new lender accepts that the existing lender has priority in terms of security. Negotiating such a deed with a bank can take a surprisingly long time – weeks, even months – and this can be very testing if cash is tight.

You can consider also whether or not you can squeeze your debtors harder and recover cash more quickly. For example, you could invoke the Late Payment of Commercial Debts (Interest) Act 1998. This gives you a statutory right to charge interest on outstanding commercial debts at the rate of 8% above the base rate. In addition, you can claim compensation ranging from £40 to £100.

Cutting expenditure

This could involve either or both of the following.

Laying off staff

This may mean that redundancy payments are triggered, and the level of payments will depend on the terms and conditions of employment of the particular individual.

If only the statutory redundancy scheme applies, then this is calculated by taking the employee's age, number of years of continuous service (minimum of two and maximum of 20 years) and the employee's gross pay (up to a maximum of £350 per week – a limit that is updated each February). In addition, the statutory notice period (or contractual notice period if higher) will need to be paid.

However, you may have agreed better redundancy terms by contract and will have to follow the contract of employment.

If you are considering making people redundant, then you must have a fair and transparent process for determining who is to be made redundant, with proper arrangements to inform and consult employees. If you do not, you could find yourself in an employment tribunal facing a claim for unfair selection for redundancy, which could give rise to much larger liabilities.

You may wish to hive off a division of the organisation. This will involve a TUPE transfer of employees as set out in the Transfer of Undertakings (Protection of Employment) Regulations 1981 (as amended). The purpose of these regulations is to protect employees' rights when the business in which they are employed is transferred to another organisation, by transferring the whole employment relationship to the transferee. There is an obligation for the transferor to inform and, where measures are to be taken in relation to employees (that is, any significant change proposed affecting an employee's terms of employment or their working conditions), to consult with the employees about the proposed transfer. The consultation period has to be a minimum of 28 days before the date of transfer. In addition, there are a number of other legal obligations on the charity as transferor, and as this can be a complex area of law – a charity contemplating such a transfer should seek legal advice.

Getting rid of onerous contracts

Can you get out of any onerous contracts, for example, a lease? It is possible that there may be break clauses that you could trigger. It is surprising how often organisations do not have a proper diary system for reminding them of the existence of break clauses, and therefore miss them. If there is no break clause, is there any chance of negotiating your way out of the contract? It is possible that a landlord might want the property back (although this is unlikely in strained economic circumstances). It is possible that you might be able to buy your way out of the contract by paying a cash sum in advance.

Fraudulent preference

Do remember, in juggling your cash flow, not to prefer one creditor over another. This is important because if a company goes into insolvent liquidation and it is held that the directors have preferred one creditor over another, then such transactions can be set aside if they were entered into six months before the onset of insolvency. This period is extended to two years where the creditor is a connected or associated person (for example, a family member).

This can be particularly difficult for charity trustees who may wish to continue supporting the charity's good works by giving money to beneficiaries, to the detriment of creditors. When insolvency looms, trustees must remember at all times that their primary duty is to the creditors and not to the charity's purpose.

Trustees of charitable companies can be held personally liable to reimburse the company for monies spent on a preferential transaction, depending on the circumstances of the case (*Re Brian Pierson (Contractors Ltd)* (2001) 1 BCLC 275).

Insurance

If you are facing the possibility that the charity is insolvent, if it is a company, the trustees need to notify the insurers of the possible risk that there could be a claim against the trustees for breach of trust or wrongful trading arising out of the charity's insolvency. Equally, if it is unincorporated, there might be allegations made that the trustees have been in breach of trust. Most trustee indemnity insurance policies cover trustees for their personal liability arising from breach of trust and wrongful trading. They do not extend to criminal liabilities arising from fraudulent trading, although they normally do cover the costs of a successful defence to a fraudulent trading charge.

Trustee indemnity insurance policies also can be particularly useful in these circumstances where claims may be made against trustees even if they are never brought to court. The trustees may need preliminary legal or professional advice to help them fight the claim and the trustee indemnity insurance policy will meet those legal costs.

However, a trustee indemnity insurance policy is not a credit insurance policy and does not cover trustees for the debts of the organisation. This is a particularly widespread misunderstanding. Many trustees of unincorporated charities think that if they have trustee indemnity insurance they will be protected against personal liability for the charity's debts: this is, of course, not true.

Conclusion

In the Charity Commission's publication *CC12 – Managing Financial Difficulties and Insolvency in Charities*, the Charity Commission states:

> Insolvency can happen overnight, for example, where a charity is dependent on grant income which is cut and not replaced by other sources of income. It may also creep up slowly over several years and remain unchecked until the charity can no longer finance its activities.

It is essential for a trustee body to have a good knowledge and understanding of the charity and its finances. Although it can be difficult to prevent the overnight collapse, even if it is anticipated, it ought to be possible to prevent or delay the onset of creeping insolvency.

The action necessary can be summed up as being 'effective management and control'. The responsibility for creating this environment rests with the trustees, but will involve all staff members whether paid or volunteers.

Lessons to learn

The financial situation that afflicts this country undoubtedly will affect a very large number of charities. The key lessons to be drawn are that to manage your way successfully through these difficult times, charity trustees need to:

- be aware of the legal structure of the charity and whether this provides limited liability

- be very realistic about assessing the charity's potential income

- ensure that the trustees really understand all the charity's commitments, liabilities and cost structures

- monitor a range of different measures to give the trustees the earliest possible warnings of dangers ahead

- act swiftly to deal with dangers when they become clear, but without panicking

- ensure that they understand the seriousness of the position and make sure that all the trustees commit enough time and energy to help deal with it.

4 Managing difficulties

Introduction

If a charity is unable to respond promptly to external factors, it may face financial difficulties and even insolvency. The first part of this chapter looks at the ways in which a charity can reverse that position by setting out the characteristics of a successful turnaround and a real-life example of where trustees had to take drastic action to save the charity.

It will not always be possible to rescue the situation and this chapter goes on to explain what the processes are if your charity does face insolvency. Finally, there is a glossary of terms used in insolvency to help you understand the detail of the processes that you may have to go through.

Managing a turnaround

A stable platform

The first question that needs to be addressed in any successful turnaround is: 'How severe is the problem?' In particular, we need to know how much breathing space we have, or how long we have before we run out of money. The important issue here is remaining in control: if we run out of money, then control may be taken from us by creditors or other stakeholders seeking to protect their position. The process of remaining in control may require a combination of deferring amounts due to creditors and obtaining short-term funding, either by selling assets or borrowing from stakeholders or funders.

At a minimum, a short-term cashflow forecast should be prepared and updated regularly. Typically, this would be a rolling weekly forecast for, say, a three-month period. Such a forecast will enable managers to identify short-term peaks in cash requirements and allow discussions to be held ahead of time to defer payments, obtain third-party funding and/or accelerate receipts wherever possible.

Retaining cash is critical in this period, so every effort to realise and conserve money needs to be made. Experience has shown that often, creditors will provide some time to allow for appropriate consideration to be given to possible turnaround options, provided that they are treated openly and consistently with other creditors. If any creditor feels that it is being 'kept at bay' while others are being paid, or that it is being told only part of the story, it is far more likely to revert to legal action and seek to recover what is owed to it.

It may be at times such as this that a charity needs to consider creative ways to conserve cash. These may include selling unnecessary assets, agreeing discounts for early settlement with debtors or diverting resources into areas that are able to generate cash, such as bringing the finalisation of a project forward to obtain funding earlier. While some of these actions may cost more in the long run, they may be justified if they maintain a stable platform in the short term to allow decisions to be taken.

A turnaround plan

Once the extent of the 'breathing space' is known, trustees will need to agree a detailed turnaround plan. This will involve making an initial assessment of the various potential options, acting decisively to rule out those which cannot be funded and concentrating only on what is achievable in the time available. Time is of the essence here. Almost by definition, the charity will have less time than is ideal to find a workable solution that is acceptable to all parties.

Obtaining a consensus among the trustees as to the viable options may be a challenge, and strong leadership will be required to ensure that the result is not inaction. This is a period when options may be unpalatable or, at best, sub-optimal. Trustees will need to understand the urgency of the situation and those with more commercial or financial expertise and experience may need to help those less experienced in such matters to arrive at an appropriate decision.

Experience also shows that information may not be easily available. Trustees will need to balance speed over accuracy or completeness of information. You could spend considerable time and some funds trying to improve the quality of the information to inform a decision. However, time and funds may be short, so you may have to make decisions with imperfect information. One frequent concern is to ensure that information relating to restricted funds is adequate to inform decisions. On the one hand, trustees will wish to be comfortable that they are not inadvertently spending restricted money. On the other hand, they will want assurance that all costs and overheads have been allocated appropriately to restricted income, such that they are not maintaining restricted funds unnecessarily which could be available for unrestricted expenditure.

Having made an assessment of all of the viable options, which may include closure of parts of the charity, redundancies, collaboration with another charity or merger, a plan needs to be developed and agreed by the trustees. This plan needs to be clear and unambiguous, supported by detailed forecasts which demonstrate that the charity can return to solvency and have regular and reviewable milestones. Like any good plan, it may include contingency plans in the event that matters do not turn out as expected.

Issues to be faced by trustees

Trustees should expect to have an enhanced level of involvement in this period, with regular meetings, conference calls and requests to review new information.

Working closely with stakeholders and funders will be vital in this period. The charity will need to conduct its affairs with openness and transparency, to ensure that stakeholders understand the full extent of the commitment that they are likely to be asked to make and can contribute to where possible. You may need to approach funders who have provided restricted funds to ask them to modify the terms of their funding so that their funds can be used to cover unrestricted expenditure, particularly if it can be demonstrated that without this, some or all of the activities may have to be closed.

In addition, keeping staff informed and motivated is very important. In particular, retaining key staff in a period of uncertainty may be challenging. Staff may wish to continue to do their best for the charity, but some may have personal circumstances which mean that they have to put their families first and find more reliable employment. You may need to give such staff incentives to remain.

We have highlighted some of the legal responsibilities of trustees in the previous chapter. Clearly, if a charity is seeking to turn itself around while it is still in financial difficulties, the trustees will need the comfort of knowing that they are not falling foul of their responsibilities and obligations. It may be wise for the trustees to seek independent personal legal advice in this regard. The advice may need to cover some of the following areas:

- insolvency law – such as the question of wrongful trading (for charities which are also limited companies)

- employment law – in the event of redundancies arising as a result of a restructuring

- property law – if a restructured operation involves relocating or vacating certain premises

- general contract law – to ensure that the charity does not inadvertently fall foul of obligations within its various operating contracts.

In addition to the above, trustees may have concerns about the difficult question of trust law, particularly surrounding the use of restricted funds. Restricted funds are held on trust for a particular purpose and therefore not available to be spent generally. You may have depleted the unrestricted funds of the charity and so can continue in the short term only by using restricted monies. This is a difficult area for trustees if such restricted funds are in fact held on trust for a particular purpose, as the trustees may be exposed to the risk that they are in 'breach of trust'. Care is needed in these circumstances and it is usually prudent to take specific legal advice in relation to the status of the restricted funds, whether the charity can use them and the risks to the trustees of so doing.

Leadership and accountability are key

It is a fact that many successful turnarounds involve changes in management. There is a strong likelihood that the management team which allowed the problems to remain unaddressed for too long may not be the right one to achieve a successful turnaround, either in reality or at least in the perception of key funders and stakeholders.

Most importantly, ownership of the turnaround plan may be a full-time job in itself. Consideration should be given to an additional, specialist interim resource with the necessary experience and authority to lead the process. There are experienced professionals in the 'situational' skills of a turnaround, including cash management, stakeholder management, decisive action, people motivation or management and strong leadership. Inevitably, there will be a cost attached to this, but external stakeholders often will respond favourably to such a change in management.

A real-life case study

This is an example of a real-life turnaround situation that illustrates many of the above points. It is a case involving a charity which was set up to further a particular religion. The charity owned premises which had an historical significance to that religion. About two years before, it had decided to open the premises as an hotel and conference venue and had set up a trading subsidiary, which in turn had contracted with a third-party company to manage the trading activity.

The charity recruited a new trustee, who quickly realised that the charity was heading towards financial difficulties and sought professional advice promptly on behalf of all the trustees. After some initial work, the following facts became apparent.

- The charity had run out of money, with creditors becoming increasingly vociferous.
- The finance department had been unable to cope with the increased activity as a result of the trading.

- The trustees did not have sufficient supervision of the trading activity to understand properly why cash was running out.
- There had been little attempt to separate the affairs of the subsidiary from those of the charity.

In short, the charity had moved from being one with limited financial activity to one that was responsible for a material trading activity, with little change to its management or governance.

The advice to the trustees was that the following urgent steps were necessary in order to achieve a stable platform from which they could take further action.

- The new trustee, now familiar with the position, was identified as the right person to take ownership of the turnaround.
- The trustees needed to obtain a valuation of the charity's premises which would assess the value of the charity's asset for different uses and in different scenarios.
- The trustees needed to approach their bank to establish the scope for short-term funding to keep creditors at bay.
- They urgently needed to make a strategic assessment of the best use of the premises.

Approval had to be sought from the Charity Commission to allow the new trustee to be paid by the charity, and she became the 'turnaround manager', with the authority and experience to make things happen quickly. The valuation of the premises suggested that there was significant value as a residential property. On the basis of this and an undertaking to prepare a clear business plan, the charity's bankers were prepared to agree a short-term overdraft to allow some of the creditors to be paid. However, the short-term cash position was still tight and needed to be managed actively on a daily basis.

This allowed for a 'breathing space' of several weeks, which gave the trustees time to consider their options. An assessment was made of the trading position of the charity. Unfortunately, financial information was less than perfect, so various assumptions had to be made in the time available. However, the available information suggested that the venue was loss-making. A decision was taken to cease to trade and a settlement deal was achieved with the management company.

This left the question of the premises: what could be done now to maximise the value of the asset to the charity, bearing in mind its historical significance?

> The key question for the trustees was: 'If you did not own the property and someone donated £X to you, would buying this property be the best way of achieving your charity's objects?'
>
> A 'no' answer suggested that it might be best to realise the property's value and use the money in a less-risky fashion. After much soul searching, the trustees agreed to sell the property, but negotiated various covenants in the sale contract to allow for access at certain times, thus preserving the charity's link with the property, but doing so without all of the expense and obligation of ownership.

Using formal insolvency processes

If it proves impossible to effect a turnaround, then managers and trustees may have no choice but to cease operations. In addition, they may have to seek some form of insolvency protection, and need to understand what processes are available to charities.

As explained in the previous chapter, many charities are constituted as companies limited by guarantee, although some will be unincorporated trusts or associations and others will be a more unusual form of legal entity, such as an industrial and provident society.

Most of the processes discussed here apply to companies limited by guarantee. Unincorporated trusts or associations will need to refer to their governing documents and different law may apply to other types of legal entity.

Overview of the main insolvency processes

In broad terms, the choice of insolvency processes for a charity that is a company limited by guarantee will depend on the answers to the three following questions.

- Is the charity insolvent?
- Is there any benefit in maintaining some or all of the charity's activities?
- Looking ahead, will the charity be able to operate at a surplus?

If the charity, in fact, remains solvent and simply needs to be wound up and to pay all of its creditors what they are due, then the charity can instigate a members' voluntary liquidation. Alternatively, the charity's trustees may elect to wind down its affairs themselves, with a view to applying to Companies House to have the charity removed from the register of companies. Often, the choice between a members' voluntary liquidation or removal from the company register will come down to the complexity of the charity's affairs and the confidence that the trustees have that nothing will emerge to render the charity insolvent.

If the charity is insolvent, then the key factor is whether there is any merit in maintaining any or all of the charity's activities as a going concern and whether there is money to pay for the costs of such activities, including wages, rent, etc. Usually, the benefit of doing so would be to protect services to beneficiaries, enhance the value of assets or reduce the possibility of increased claims for damages as a result of early termination of contracts. It may be possible also to transfer certain activities to another charity.

If there is merit in maintaining some of the activities, then the best process may well be administration. This provides a freeze on the ability of creditors to take action to recover their debts and allows the administrator to continue to operate the charity as a going concern, with a view to maximising returns for the charity's creditors. It is possible that receivership might achieve the same end, in the event that the charity has borrowing supported by a charge over its assets, although this is likely to be a rare occurrence.

If the charity is able to operate at a surplus going forward, either through a restructuring of its activities or because the factors which gave rise to the insolvent position will not recur, then it may be in a position to make an offer to pay its creditors less than 100% in full and final settlement. Such an offer may be more attractive to creditors than having the charity wound up, in which case assets may lose their value and additional creditors' claims may arise, which may lead to a much lower return for creditors than is being offered.

Such an offer can be made without recourse to a formal insolvency process, particularly if there are only a small number of creditors. Alternatively, the charity may seek to enter into a company voluntary arrangement (CVA), which is a formal process designed to allow an offer for settlement to be made, such that it binds all creditors, provided that a sufficient majority (in essence 75% by value) agree to the proposed settlement.

If none of the above is possible and the charity must cease its affairs, then it is likely that the charity will wish to enter into creditors' voluntary liquidation (CVL). In this case, the liquidator will have a duty to maximise the amount realised for creditors, and their ability to continue the charity's affairs is more limited than that of an administrator.

Common questions answered

What is insolvency?

A company becomes insolvent if it does not have enough assets to cover its debts and/or it cannot pay its debts on the due dates. It is the directors' (that is, the trustees') responsibility to know whether or not the company is trading while insolvent and they can be held legally responsible for continuing to trade in that situation (see Wrongful trading).

What formal insolvency procedures are open to an insolvent company?

These fall into five main categories. The first three provide the potential for the rescue of the company or its activities, while the last two do not:

- administration
- CVA
- administrative receiverships
- compulsory liquidation
- CVL.

What is administration?

The administration procedure, first introduced in the Insolvency Act 1986 and substantially revised by the Enterprise Act 2002, is designed to hold a business together while plans are formed either to put in place a financial restructuring to rescue the company, or to sell the business and assets to produce a better result for creditors than a liquidation. Administration also can be used where neither of these objectives can be achieved, simply as a mechanism to liquidate assets and distribute the proceeds to secured or preferential creditors, but this is not the primary purpose of administration.

A company can go into administration in a number of ways. The company is then placed under the day-to-day control and management of administrators, who will be insolvency practitioners. It is their responsibility to formulate proposals and present these to the creditors to vote on them.

Once a company is placed in administration it is protected, and no creditor can take steps (without the administrator's agreement or the court's permission) to recover any assets or take certain other actions against the company.

How does rescuing the company differ from rescuing the business?

A rescue of the company through an insolvency process may happen through a CVA, which often is preceded by administration in order to protect the company while the rescue takes place. The CVA usually will involve creditors writing off part of their debt in order to restore the company to solvency, which in turn preserves some value for the charity and enables control to be handed back to the directors (trustees).

A business is rescued through an insolvency process where the insolvency practitioner, whether an administrative receiver or administrator, negotiates a sale of the business and assets to a new company. Generally, employment contracts are automatically transferred by law to the new company, but other contracts remain with the old company. The new company will negotiate new trading relationships with customers and suppliers, and the insolvency practitioner in the old company distributes the sale proceeds to the creditors in accordance with their legal entitlements.

What types of receivership are there?

There are two main relevant types of receivership.

- **Fixed charge receivership:** this is a process where the holder of a fixed charge over a specific asset (for example, a property) appoints a receiver to realise that asset only. A fixed charge receiver need not be an insolvency practitioner and has no general power of management of the business. Where the appointment is over a property, the fixed charge receiver is sometimes known as an LPA receiver, because the appointment takes place under the terms of the Law of Property Act 1925. This process is only available in England and Wales.

- **Administrative receivership:** an administrative receiver is appointed under a charge that covers all or most of the company's assets, including its goodwill. This type of charge is referred to as a floating charge or debenture. The holder of the charge, that is, the lender, is referred to often as the debenture holder. This may be one lender or sometimes a consortium of lenders.

Since September 2003, the Enterprise Act 2002 introduced restrictions on the ability of floating charge holders to appoint administrative receivers.

In Scotland, this type of receivership is known simply as receivership and the charge is referred to as a bond and floating charge, not a debenture.

It may seem as if the receiver is simply a debt collector for the lender who appointed them and to whom they have a primary duty, with a few legal obligations to people such as preferential creditors. In fact, the receiver will seek to obtain the best value for all creditors, although not at the floating charge holder's expense.

The receiver can continue trading and often will do so – at least for a limited period – in the hope of selling the business as a going concern. If successful, this usually will achieve a higher price than one would get by breaking up the assets. It also gives the business a chance to survive and succeed under new management. If the business is sold, the buyer receives the business free of debt and the money goes to the receiver to distribute to secured and preferential creditors. (Only a liquidator may distribute any remaining funds to unsecured creditors.)

What is the difference between receivership and administration?

Administrative receivers are appointed by the lender (or a consortium of lenders) who holds security in the form of a floating charge. Administrators are appointed either by the court, on the application of the company, directors or creditors, or out of court by floating charge holders or the company or directors. Their role is to take charge of the company temporarily while proposals are drafted for approval by creditors and then to manage the property, affairs and business of the company in accordance with the approved proposals. These proposals may be either for the restructuring of the company's debts before returning it to the directors' control, or the realisation of the assets of the company. Both processes are available to floating charge holders who had existing floating charges prior to 15 September 2003; whether a floating charge holder opts for receivership or administration will depend on the circumstances of each case. However, for floating charge holders whose charges were not created prior to 15 September 2003, administrative receivership is no longer an option in most cases.

The primary duty of a receiver is to recover the debt due to the holder of the charge who appointed them, although they have certain overriding duties to all creditors (for example, a duty to get a proper price for the assets). An administrator is an officer of the court no matter who appointed them and has a duty to all creditors.

What is a company voluntary arrangement?

A CVA is an insolvency procedure. It is a renegotiation of the payments due to all of a company's creditors, or some other form of financial restructuring, and is subject to a creditors' meeting and vote. A CVA must be supervised by a licensed insolvency practitioner, who acts as the nominee, pending the approval of the arrangement, and usually becomes the supervisor once it comes into effect. A proposal for a CVA also can be made by an administrator or liquidator.

In addition, companies may reach an informal arrangement with their creditors, for example to seek more time to pay their debts. Such an arrangement may be with a small number of creditors, although if the arrangement is proposed to extend to a large number of creditors, the need for the protection of a formal insolvency process is greater.

What is liquidation?

As the word suggests, liquidation means turning a company's assets into cash and then distributing this to the creditors. It is the most commonly used procedure for insolvent companies, and is the end of the road for a company. After the assets are sold and the proceeds distributed, the company is struck off the register, or dissolved. It literally ceases to exist. Most companies that go into insolvent liquidation have stopped trading already and therefore it is very unusual for a liquidator to be able to carry on the business. Even where a company is still trading when it goes into insolvent liquidation, the liquidator rarely will continue to trade in the hope of salvaging something of the business because their powers to do so are limited.

There are different types of liquidation. In a members' voluntary liquidation (solvent liquidation) the company is able to pay its debts in full, together with interest. This may arise when the charity has fulfilled its purpose or can no longer justify continuing, and the directors or trustees decide that any surplus of assets is better placed in the hands of another charity.

Insolvent liquidation, which entails the distribution of assets to creditors who will not be paid in full, can arise in several ways. It may follow from receivership or administration as a vehicle for distributing funds. Or, recognising that it is insolvent, the company itself may resolve to go into liquidation (CVL). Finally, a court can make a winding-up order (compulsory liquidation) on the petition of an unpaid creditor or the company itself, its directors or shareholders.

A liquidator should act in the best interests of all creditors. When they follow a receiver they also will review the acts of the receiver (for example, check the validity of the receiver's appointment and ensure that the receiver has disposed of the assets under their control properly).

Who appoints liquidators?

In a CVL the members pass a resolution (typically a 75% majority is required) to wind up the company and appoint a liquidator, who must be a licensed insolvency practitioner. The creditors then meet and either confirm the liquidator's appointment or appoint another one of their choosing. Voting is by a majority (by value) of creditors.

Apart from a couple of rare technical exceptions, compulsory liquidation is the only insolvency procedure which *any* creditor can instigate unilaterally, regardless of the company's wishes. In all other procedures, the company has to participate to some extent in the process. Therefore, it tends to be a last resort for frustrated creditors when the company cannot or will not cooperate in any other procedure.

The creditor starts the process by petitioning the court for a winding-up order. This will be made as long as the court is satisfied that the creditor is owed more than £750 and that the company is insolvent. In most cases, insolvency can be established by the creditor issuing a statutory demand for payment and the company failing to pay the debt demanded within 21 days.

What is the order of payment out of assets in an insolvency process?

Any individual or organisation holding a fixed charge over a company's assets is paid first out of the sale proceeds of those assets (after the costs of realisation). Then, after the payment of other costs and expenses, the second group to receive funds, if there are any left, are preferential creditors. Preferential creditors primarily comprise employees' claims for arrears of pay or accrued holiday pay, and unpaid contributions to occupational pension schemes and state scheme premiums, all within certain specified limits. Then, if there is a floating charge created on or after 15 September 2003, a proportion of the remaining funds (called the prescribed part), subject to a maximum of £600,000, is made available for unsecured creditors. Next comes any creditor with a floating charge. Fourth in line are unsecured creditors, and finally any surplus is available to pass to a charity with similar objectives.

What happens to the employees of an insolvent company?

The fate of the employees is determined largely by the type of procedure that is used for the insolvent company. If the company is rescued, or all or part of the business is sold as a going concern, the jobs of the employees working in the business at the time of rescue or sale may be saved.

If, however, employees are made redundant as part of the process, the government will meet various employee entitlements, subject to limits which are periodically revised. These claims are all paid by the Department for Business, Enterprise & Regulatory Reform (BERR), which then claims as a creditor in the insolvency for the sums paid out. Often these payments will not compensate employees for all of their entitlements and therefore they are left to claim the balance against the insolvent company. Employees are entitled to claim arrears of pay and/or holiday pay as preferential creditors, subject to certain limits. The balance of all of their entitlements, including payment in lieu of notice, statutory redundancy pay and any other contractual entitlements, will rank as an unsecured creditor.

What happens to the directors of an insolvent company?

Very little happens by way of an automatic process – much depends on the type of insolvency. In a liquidation, a director will have no continuing role in managing the company, but in an administration, administrative receivership or CVA they may have. If they have given personal guarantees to any creditors, they may be called upon to pay them. A director is usually also an employee of the company, and is subject to the same processes and claims as employees generally.

Is the conduct of directors automatically investigated?

In all cases other than voluntary arrangements and solvent liquidations, the insolvency practitioner has a duty to report to BERR on the conduct of each director (up to three years before the date of insolvency) to help BERR to determine whether disqualification proceedings should be started. Except in liquidations, this report is based on information that is brought to the insolvency practitioner's attention, and BERR is not required to make a general investigation into the director's dealings. In general, only a liquidator in an insolvent liquidation has a duty to investigate the conduct of directors.

Glossary

Administration One of the main corporate insolvency procedures, it can be a precursor to a company voluntary arrangement (CVA) under which the company is restructured and passed back to its directors. In an administration, the insolvency practitioner, as officer of the court, takes over powers of management of the business (but is able to delegate these back to management). Their objective is to rescue the company, or if that is not possible or the result would be better for creditors, to achieve a better result for creditors than a liquidation (often through rescuing the business as a going concern) and provide protection from actions by creditors while doing so. A partnership also can be subject to administration and this can be as a prelude to a partnership voluntary arrangement.

Administrative receiver (in Scotland, simply 'a receiver') Insolvency practitioner appointed in an administrative receivership. The administrative receiver is commonly known as the 'receiver' – not to be confused with the official receiver.

Administrative receivership (usually shortened to 'receivership') Non-court procedure whereby an insolvency practitioner takes control of the whole of a company's assets under the terms of a lender's floating charge.

Administrator Insolvency practitioner appointed in an administration.

Charge A security held by the lender over the assets of a borrower.

Company voluntary arrangement (CVA) A formal proposal by the directors for payment in full or in part of their company's debts. If the company is in liquidation or administration, either the liquidator or the administrator may put forward such proposals. It is a rescue procedure aimed at preserving the company and maximising the potential dividend for creditors.

Compulsory liquidation A liquidation brought about by order of court, usually because an unpaid creditor petitions the court having exhausted all other remedies. In

England and Wales, the official receiver first takes control, but if there are assets to pay the costs, an insolvency practitioner may be appointed later by creditors or by the Secretary of State. In Scotland, an interim liquidator is always appointed at the same time as a winding-up order is granted. However, an interim appointment may be preceded by the appointment of a provisional liquidator if the court decides that it is appropriate.

Creditor A person owed money.

Creditors' voluntary liquidation (CVL) Winding-up of an insolvent company, brought about by a resolution of shareholders. At a subsequent creditors' meeting, the liquidator either will be confirmed in office or replaced by the creditors' choice.

Debenture This term has no precise meaning. One definition is a document acknowledging a debt, usually issued by a company. Debentures may be secured or unsecured, but the term is used commonly to describe a document containing a floating charge and possibly also some sort of fixed security.

Debtor A person owing money.

Disqualification On application to the court by the Department for Business, Enterprise & Regulatory Reform, a director found guilty of unfit conduct may be disqualified from holding any management position in a company for between two and 15 years. Alternatively a director may be disqualified by giving a disqualification undertaking to the Secretary of State, which has the same effect as a disqualification order by the court.

Enterprise Act 2002 Legislation intended to facilitate company rescue and the swift rehabilitation of debtors. The Act introduced a streamlined administration procedure, and faster rehabilitation for bankrupts by importing new and revised sections into the Insolvency Act 1986, which remains the primary piece of legislation for UK insolvency.

Fixed charge Security over specific assets, such as goodwill, property or shares. No fixed charge can be created in Scotland other than over property assets. Such a charge is referred to in Scotland as a Standard Security.

Fixed charge receiver A receiver, who need not be an insolvency practitioner, appointed by the holder of a fixed charge to realise the charged asset.

Floating charge An equitable charge on property that may change from time to time in the ordinary course of business (for example, stock). Such a charge can be converted (or crystallised) into a fixed charge over those assets.

Going concern Basis on which insolvency practitioners prefer to sell a business. Effectively it means the business continues, jobs are saved and a higher price is obtained.

Insolvency Defined alternatively as having insufficient assets to meet all debts, or being unable to pay debts as and when they fall due. If a creditor can establish either test, they will be able to present a winding-up petition (in England and Wales or Scotland) or a bankruptcy petition (in England and Wales) as long as the debt is more than £750. In Scotland, the creditor's debt must be at least £3,000 to present a petition for sequestration.

Insolvency Act 1986 Primary legislation governing insolvency law and practice. Nevertheless, many other statutes are also relevant.

Insolvency practitioner A person authorised (licensed) by one of the recognised professional bodies to act in insolvency matters, including the winding-up of a solvent company. Insolvency practitioners must pass an examination before they are able to apply for a licence.

Judgment Recognition of a debt by a court or the decision given by a court at the conclusion of a trial.

Liquidation Process that eventually brings a company's existence to an end after distributing its assets to creditors/shareholders.

Liquidator The official receiver or licensed insolvency practitioner appointed to wind up the affairs of a company.

LPA receiver (Law of Property Act 1925 receiver) A person, not necessarily an insolvency practitioner, appointed to take charge of a mortgaged property or other asset by a lender whose loan is in default. In practice, often this term is (inaccurately) used interchangeably with fixed charge receiver.

Member In relation to an insolvent company, a member is a shareholder or subscriber. In relation to an insolvent partnership in England and Wales, it is any partner in the partnership.

Members' voluntary liquidation (solvent liquidation) Winding-up of a company that is able to pay its debts in full, together with interest. Surplus assets are distributed to shareholders (members) The liquidation must still be carried out by a licensed insolvency practitioner.

Nominee Title given to an insolvency practitioner acting in a voluntary arrangement, prior to the creditors approving (or rejecting) the scheme. Occasionally used in the non-technical sense (e.g. 'ABC Limited is going for administration with Mr X as the nominee', meaning that he is the proposed administrator).

Official receiver The government department responsible, among other matters, for acting as liquidator in compulsory liquidations.

Petition A document presented to the court to request the commencement of compulsory liquidation or bankruptcy. The document used to request an administration order is called an application.

Preferential creditor A creditor given special rights as a matter of public policy, to be paid ahead of the ordinary creditors. Preferential status for certain Crown debts such as PAYE, NIC, VAT was abolished by the Enterprise Act 2002, and preferential debts are now restricted (with some obscure exceptions) to employees' claims for arrears of pay and accrued holiday pay, and unpaid pension contributions in certain circumstances.

Prescribed part Introduced by the Enterprise Act 2002, this is an amount set aside out of floating charge assets, to be made available to unsecured creditors. It only applies in insolvencies where there is a floating charge created on or after 15 September 2003.

Receiver/receivership See administrative receiver/receivership.

Secured creditor A creditor with security over some or all of the debtor's assets. In essence, a secured creditor is paid before ordinary creditors.

Security A charge (which may be a fixed charge or a floating charge) or mortgage over assets taken to secure repayment of a debt. If the debt is not paid, the lender may have a right to sell the charged assets and/or the right to appoint a receiver (or administrator, if the charge is a floating charge over substantially the whole of the debtor's assets).

Sequestration Term used for a personal bankruptcy under the Bankruptcy (Scotland) Act 1985. The process differs from an English bankruptcy in significant respects.

Solvent liquidation See members' voluntary liquidation.

Statutory demand A formal notice requiring payment of a debt within 21 days, in default of which bankruptcy proceedings may be commenced against an individual by a creditor without further notice in England and Wales provided the debt is at least £750. In Scotland, sequestration proceedings may be commenced by a creditor without further notice provided the debt is at least £3,000. Alternatively, such a notice can be served on a company and, in default of payment, liquidation proceedings may be commenced by the creditor without further notice in England and Wales or Scotland, provided that the debt exceeds £750.

Supervisor Title given to an insolvency practitioner appointed in a voluntary arrangement, whether for an individual or a company or partnership.

Unsecured creditor Strictly, any creditor who does not hold security. More commonly used to refer to any ordinary creditor who has no preferential rights, although, in fact, preferential creditors invariably will be unsecured. In any event, almost the last in the queue, ahead only of shareholders.

Voluntary liquidation A liquidation initiated by the company, not one imposed by the court. It may be a members' voluntary liquidation (solvent) or a creditors' voluntary liquidation (insolvent).

Winding-up order Order made by the court for a company to be placed into compulsory liquidation.

Wrongful trading When a company continues to trade beyond the point where insolvent liquidation becomes inevitable and further losses to creditors occur after that point. The directors may be personally liable for the losses unless they have taken 'every step' to minimise those losses. No criminal or fraudulent intent is necessary.

Index

accounting
   going concern basis 64
accounting standards
   FRS 18 *Accounting policies* 64
Action for Children 46
administration 87, 88
   comparison with receivership 90
   definition 93
   directors' fate 92
administrative costs
   review of 33–5
administrator
   definition 93
Allford, Marion 58
assets
   definition 39
auditing standards
   going concern test 65

bad debt
   definition 39
balance sheet
   terminology 39–40
   test for insolvency 62–5
bank loans
   dealing with cash flow crisis 77
bank overdraft
   cashflow management 38, 61
Bennett, Margaret 52
breach of trust 70–1
buildings
   review of premises costs 33

Cards for Good Causes 55
cashflow
   borrowing 38
   credit control 38
   forecasting 30–2, 40
   management 37–8
   test for insolvency 61–2

charitable companies
   breach of trust 70–1
   effect of insolvency 60–1, 65
   fraudulent trading 68
   implications for trustees of looming insolvency 71–2
   wrongful trading 7, 68–70
charitable companies limited by guarantee
   insolvency, effect of 6, 60–1, 67–71, 76
charitable trust *see* trusts
charities
   legal status 6, 60
Charities Act 1993 60, 65, 67, 70–1, 73, 74
Charities Act 2006 77
Charity Aid Foundation Venturesome Fund 77
Charity Commission 1
   applications for charitable incorporated organisations to start from April 2010 76
   CC12 *Managing Financial Difficulties and Insolvencies in Charities* 73, 79–80
   inquiry into breach of trust 70–1
Christian Aid 48
Civil Liability (Contribution) Act 1978 66
Clay, Anthony 50
Comic Relief 48
communication
   fundraising, channels for 48
Companies Act 2006 70
companies limited by guarantee
   insolvency, effect of 6, 60–1, 67–71, 76
   insolvency procedure 86–7
Company Directors' Disqualification Act 1986 70
company voluntary arrangement (CVA) 87
   directors' fate 92
   meaning 90, 93

INDEX

compulsory liquidation 91
   definition 93–4
consortium bids 36
contingency planning 18
core business focus 5, 48–50
corporate fundraising
   during recession 56–8
costs
   risk management 13–15
   variable 14–15, 41
credit control 38
credit crunch
   impact on charities 1
credit terms 38
creditors
   definition 39, 94
creditors' voluntary liquidation (CVL) 87, 89, 91
   appointment of liquidators 91
   definition 94
current assets
   definition 40
current liabilities
   definition 40

debt collection 38
debtors
   definition 40, 94
Department for Business, Enterprise & Regulatory Reform 92, 93
depreciation
   definition 40
designated funds 19
   definition 39
   insolvency, treatment in 75
digital media
   fundraising with aid of 43, 48, 55–6
directors
   disqualification 70, 93, 94
   fraudulent trading 68
   impact of insolvency 92–3
   liability 68–70
   report on conduct prior insolvency 93
   wrongful trading 69–70
disqualification 70, 93
   definition 94
donors
   core donor group 44, 49
   development 53–4
   online 55–6

downturn *see* credit crunch; recession

employees
   fraudulent trading 68
   impact of insolvency 92
employment law
   redundancy 77–8, 92
   Transfer of Undertakings (Protection of Employment) Regulations 1981 (TUPE) 78
endowment funds 19
   definition 39
   expendable endowment 73
   permanent endowment 73
Enterprise Act 2002 88, 89, 94
expenses
   review of commitments 22–3

failure
   charities 1–2
financial management
   effective 2–4, 9–41
financial statements
   going concern basis 64–5
   terminology 39–40
   see also balance sheet
fixed assets
   definition 40
fixed costs
   definition 40
   review of 33–5
   risk management 13
fraudulent trading 68
FRS 18 *Accounting policies* 64
fundraisers
   investment in 47
   nurturing expertise 5, 46–7
fundraising
   communication channels 48
   core donor group 44, 49
   corporate 56–8
   digital media, using 43, 48, 55–6
   grants 58–9
   innovation 55–6
   investment in programmes 54–5
   regular giving 43
   selective pruning of programmes 50–1
   standing out from the crowd 47–8
   strategy during recession 4–6, 52–9

funds
- designated 19, 39, 75
- endowment 19, 39, 73
- general 19–20, 39, 51–2
- reserves 19–20, 39
- restricted 19, 39, 73–5
- terminology 39
- unrestricted 19–20, 39

general funds 19–20, 51–2
- definition 39

glossary
- balance sheet items 39–40
- funds of a charity 39
- management information terms 40–1

going concern
- accounting on a going concern basis 64
- auditing standard 65
- charity in administration 87
- definition 94
- test for insolvency 61–2

grant funding
- fundraising 58–9
- terms and conditions 75
- whether separate grants constitute special trusts 74–5

Gray, John 46

income
- committed versus ad hoc giving 51
- confirmed 17–18
- possible 18
- probable 18
- review of future streams 20–2
- sources 18, 20–2
- uncertain 18
- voluntary 17–18

indemnity clauses 65–6

indemnity insurance
- trustees 66–7, 79

Individual Giving 52

Industrial and Provident Societies Act 1965 60, 68

innovation
- fundraising 55–6

insolvency
- administration procedure 87, 88
- balance sheet test 62–5
- *Re Brian Pierson (Contractors Ltd)* preferential transaction case 79

Re Cheyne Finance plc (In Receivership) case 61–2

Re A Company No.001418 fraudulent trading case 68

company voluntary arrangement (CVA) procedure 87, 89, 90

conduct of directors 93

creditors' voluntary liquidation (CVL) procedure 87, 89, 91

definition 88, 95

designated funds, treatment of 75

directors' fate 92–3

effect on different legal structures 6–7, 60–1, 65–71, 76

employees' fate 92

endowment funds, treatment of 73

fraudulent preference 78–9

fraudulent trading 68

glossary of terms 93–7

going concern test 61–2

Re Grantham fraudulent trading case 68

implications for trustees of looming insolvency 71–2

informing insurers 79

limited companies 60–1, 65

managing through a crisis 76–9

members' voluntary liquidation procedure 86–7, 91

Norman v Theodore Goddard on trustee's standard of care 70

order of payment out of assets 92

practical implications 7, 71–2

preferential creditors 92, 96

procedures for a company limited by guarantee 86–93

Re Produce Marketing Consortium Ltd wrongful trading case 69

restricted funds, treatment of 7, 73–5

special trusts, treatment of 74–5

tests 6, 61–5

trusts, treatment of 7, 60–1, 65–7

unincorporated associations 60–1, 67

Re White and Osmond (Parkstone) Ltd 'sunshine test' 69

wrongful trading 7, 68–70

Insolvency Act 1986 60–1, 88, 95
- balance sheet test 62
- fraudulent trading 68
- going concern test 61

wrongful trading 68, 69
insolvency practitioner 95
insurance
   insolvency implications 79
investments
   definition 40

key performance indicators (KPIs) 24–5
   definition 40–1
   lag indicators 24, 40
   lead indicators 25, 41

Late Payment of Commercial Debt
   (Interest) Act 1998 77
Law of Property Act 1925 89
   LPA receiver 95
leadership 8
   case study 84–6
   turnaround, in a 84
liabilities
   definition 40
limited companies
   effect of insolvency 60–1, 65
   implications for trustees of looming
     insolvency 71–2
limited liability organisations *see* companies
   limited by guarantee
liquidation
   appointment of liquidators 91
   directors' fate 92
   meaning 91, 95
loans
   cashflow management 38
   dealing with cash flow crisis 77
LPA receiver 95

management information 4, 24–38
   cashflow forecasting, use for 30–2
   key performance indicators 24–5
   restricted expenditure, use for monitoring
     25–8
   terminology 40–1
   unrestricted income, use for monitoring
     28–9
members' voluntary liquidation 86–7, 91
   definition 95
mergers 36–7
   financial difficulties, consideration during
     37
   reasons for 36

national insurance contributions
   cashflow management 37–8
negligence
   breach of trust 70–1
   directors' liability 68–70
   exoneration under Companies Act 2006
     70
   wrongful trading 69–70
nominee 95
non-executive directors
   wrongful trading 70
NSPCC 44, 48

official receiver 95
onerous contracts
   release from 78
online donors 55–6
overhead costs
   review of 33–5

partnerships
   corporate fundraising 56–8
Pegram, Giles 44
performance-related grants 27, 41
permanent endowment
   treatment in case of insolvency 73
petition 95
portfolio management 48–52
preferential creditor 92, 96
premises
   review of costs 33
prescribed part 96
property
   review of premises costs 33

receivership
   administrative receivership 89
   comparison with administration 90
   directors' fate 92
   fixed charge receivership 89
   types 89–90
recession
   embracing change during 44–5
   fundraising strategy during 4–6,
     52–9
   media 'hype' 42
   'tuning in' during 45–6
redundancy
   law 77–8, 92
   reducing staff costs 77–8

reserves 19–20
　assessment of level 23–4
　definition 39
reserves policy 3–4
　review of 19–24
restricted funds
　definition 19, 39
　insolvency, treatment in 7, 73–5
　monitoring expenditure 25–8
　turnaround, use in a 83–4
　whether constituting a special trust 74–5
Rich, Judith 55
risk assessment 3, 13–18
　fixed costs 13–14
　variable costs 14–15
　voluntary income, assessing certainty 17–18
RSPB 50

salaries
　review of 33–4
scenario planning 3, 10–13
sequestration 96
shadow directors
　wrongful trading 69–70
social networking 55
special trusts
　definition 74
　examples 74
　expendable endowment 73
　insolvency, treatment in 74–5
staff costs
　reducing through redundancy 77–8
　review of 33–4
staff investment 47
statutory demand 96
strategic management 3, 9–13

tax payments
　cashflow management 37–8
Transfer of Undertakings (Protection of Employment) Regulations 1981 (TUPE) 78

trustees
　breach of trust 70–1
　disqualification 70
　fraudulent trading 68
　implications of looming insolvency 71–2
　indemnity clauses 65–6
　indemnity insurance 66–7, 79
　joint and several liability 66
　managing through an insolvency crisis 76–9
　turnaround, involvement in 83–4
　wrongful trading 70
trusts
　indemnity clauses 65–6
　insolvency, effect of 7, 60–1, 65–7
　joint and several liability 66
　Knight v Knight 'three certainties' test 75
　trustee indemnity insurance 66–7, 79
　see also special trusts
turnaround
　leadership 84
　management 81–6
　plan 8, 82–3

unincorporated associations
　effect of insolvency 60–1, 67
　implications for trustees of looming insolvency 71
　insolvency procedure 86
　see also trusts
unrestricted funds 19–20
　definition 39
　monitoring income 28–9

variable costs 14–15
　definition 41
VAT payments
　cashflow management 38

winding-up order 91, 97
Wishing Well Appeal for Great Ormond Street Children's Hospital 58
wrongful trading 68–70
　meaning 7, 97